WEALTH:

THE HEALTHCARE MILLIONAIRE

Hardcover ISBN: 9798295755071

WEALTH:

THE HEALTHCARE MILLIONAIRE

ESSENTIAL TOOLS FOR BUILDING RICHES

SHAKEEL AHMED, M.D.

"And the day came when the risk to remain tight in a bud
was more painful than the risk it took to blossom"
—- Anais Nin

TABLE OF CONTENTS

PROLOGUE

"If people knew how hard I worked to get my mastery,
it wouldn't seem so wonderful at all."
—Michelangelo

For years, I sat in the physician's chair believing in a simple, almost sacred equation: I provide a necessary service, and in return, I am fairly compensated. It was a linear, comfortable way of looking at the world. It made perfect sense as a clinician, but it kept me blind to the reality of healthcare as an economic system. I assumed that if I stayed disciplined, maximized my billing, and avoided the "stupidity" of flashy liabilities, the math of a high salary would eventually tip the scales toward freedom.

I was wrong. The realization didn't come all at once, but through a slow, uncomfortable settling of the facts: no matter how skilled I was or how much revenue I generated, I was still the product—and products are eventually replaced or phased out. High income is not wealth; it is a seductive treadmill that only moves as long as you keep running.

This book is the result of my shift from thinking like a clinician to thinking like an owner. It is about moving beyond the "labor stack" to understand the "value stack" where real money moves and stays. I am not interested in offering shortcuts or a menu of generic stock picks. I am here to map the actual terrain, demystify the formulas, and arm you with the systemic knowledge required to own the game rather than just being played by it. We are going to stop looking at the scoreboard and start looking at how the league is run. As Garry Kasparov said, "You don't win by explaining the rules. You win by mastering them."

CHAPTER 1

WHY MEDICINE MAKES MILLIONAIRES (AND WHY MOST DOCTORS NEVER BECOME ONE)

"When written in Chinese, the word 'crisis' is composed of two characters—one represents danger, and the other represents opportunity."
— John F. Kennedy

Medicine is one of the most powerful wealth-producing industries ever created. I have watched it remain stable, recession-resistant, politically protected, and structurally permanent throughout my career. People do not stop getting sick during downturns. Governments do not allow healthcare systems to fail. Insurance companies guarantee payment streams. Demand rises every year with aging populations, chronic disease, and technological expansion. Very few industries combine inevitability, scale, and protection the way healthcare does.

And yet, despite sitting at the center of this economic machine, I have seen most physicians never build meaningful wealth.

In the United States, physicians consistently rank among the highest earners in the workforce. Median physician compensation across all specialties exceeds $350,000 per year. Procedural specialists routinely earn $500,000 to $700,000 annually, with some orthopedic, spine, cardiology, and interventional subspecialties crossing seven figures. Over a 30-year career, I know a physician will often generate between $10 and $25 million in gross professional revenue through personal labor alone.

Those numbers should produce extraordinary wealth.

They usually do not.

Multiple national surveys paint a sobering picture. Roughly 45–50% of physicians reach their late 50s with a net worth below $1 million. Nearly one in four physicians report living paycheck to paycheck at some point in their careers. More than half delay retirement beyond their planned age, not because they want to work longer, but because they cannot afford not to. Burnout rates exceed 60%, and financial stress consistently ranks among the top drivers—alongside administrative burden, declining reimbursement, and loss of professional autonomy.

This disconnect is not about intelligence, discipline, or effort. I believe physicians are among the most educated, credentialed, and hardworking professionals in society. The problem is structural, not personal.

Healthcare itself is a financial juggernaut. The U.S. healthcare economy now exceeds $4.5 trillion annually, accounting for approximately 18% of GDP—larger than the economies of Germany or Japan. Healthcare spending has grown faster than inflation for decades and is projected to approach $6 trillion within the next ten years. Every year, I watch massive wealth being created inside this system.

Hospital systems report annual revenues in the tens of billions. Publicly traded healthcare companies routinely post double-digit margins. Private equity firms deploy hundreds of billions of dollars into healthcare platforms, acquiring practices, surgery centers, laboratories, imaging networks, pharmacies, and management companies. Healthcare remains one of the most targeted sectors for institutional capital because its cash flows are predictable, defensible, and scalable.

Millionaires and billionaires are created every year in healthcare.

Just not at the bedside.

The core problem is participation. I see physicians participate almost exclusively as labor. They generate revenue but rarely own the infrastructure that captures it.

From the first day of medical school, I was taught—and watched others taught—to think in terms of income. Success is framed as compensation: salary offers, collections, RVUs, productivity bonuses, partnership tracks. The implicit promise is simple—work harder, earn more. For a time, this model works. Early in a career, rising income feels like progress. The jump from residency to attending pay feels transformative. The first few years of practice create the illusion that wealth is inevitable.

Then the ceiling appears.

Income has limits. Time has limits. Physical and emotional endurance have limits. I know a physician can only see so many patients, perform so many procedures, or take so much call. Even at the highest pay rates, the model remains linear: more work equals more money, less work equals less money. There is no leverage.

At the same time, the largest financial gains in healthcare occur far from the exam room.

Ownership is the dividing line.

Hospitals generate revenue 24 hours a day regardless of which physician is on call. Surgery centers earn facility fees whether or not the operating surgeon owns equity. Laboratories process thousands of tests daily with minimal marginal cost per additional test. Imaging centers bill high-value studies while expensive equipment depreciates aggressively for tax purposes. Pharmacies generate recurring margin with every refill, month after month, year after year. These businesses scale. Labor does not.

The financial contrast is stark. I have seen a physician earning $500,000 annually pay an effective tax rate exceeding 40% once federal, state, payroll, and Medicare taxes are accounted for. That same physician owning equity in a healthcare facility may reduce their effective rate dramatically through depreciation, interest deductions, cost segregation, and long-term capital gains treatment. Over a career, the difference can amount to millions of dollars in retained capital.

Meanwhile, non-physician investors understand this distinction intuitively. Private equity firms do not chase income. They chase assets. They buy infrastructure, consolidate fragmented markets, standardize operations, and apply leverage. Hospital systems focus on facility control, downstream referrals, and payer dominance. Insurers design networks to capture margin across the entire care continuum. Physicians, ironically, generate the revenue that makes these strategies viable but rarely participate meaningfully in the upside.

This imbalance explains why two physicians with identical incomes can end their careers in radically different financial positions. I have watched one retire with passive cash flow, optionality, and negotiating power. I have watched another work longer than planned, scale back lifestyle expectations, and wonder where decades of earnings went. The difference is not how much they earned. It is what they owned.

Even savings discipline is not enough. I have seen a physician who saves 20% of a $400,000 salary for 30 years accumulate a respectable retirement portfolio. But that portfolio is still constrained by market returns, taxation, inflation, and sequence risk. It does not offer control. It does not offer leverage. It does not compound the way ownership does.

Consider where real wealth accumulates in healthcare. Facility ownership routinely produces annual returns that exceed physician salaries. Ancillary services often generate margins two to three times higher than professional fees. Consolidated platforms trade at EBITDA multiples far above those of individual practices. Exit events—sales, recapitalizations, mergers—create liquidity events that dwarf decades of clinical income.

This is why private equity continues to outbid physicians for healthcare assets. I understand that they see medicine not just as a profession, but as an ecosystem. And ecosystems reward those who control infrastructure, not those who merely pass through it.

None of this requires abandoning clinical medicine. In fact, I believe clinical expertise is often the entry point. Physicians have credibility, access, and operational insight that outside investors lack. But without intentional movement toward ownership, those advantages are squandered.

The uncomfortable truth is this: medicine does not make doctors wealthy by default. It makes owners wealthy.

Doctors are taught how to diagnose disease, not how to diagnose financial structure. I was trained to manage risk in patients, not in capital. Physicians are encouraged to be conservative with money, even when conservatism carries its own hidden risks. Over time, this mindset produces high earners who remain financially fragile.

Wealth in healthcare is created downstream from clinical work—after the patient encounter ends. It accumulates where billing is multiplied, overhead is shared, margins are protected, and capital is deployed strategically. It rewards structure, patience, and ownership far more than effort alone.

Once this reality is understood, medicine stops being merely a high-paying job. I see it become something far more powerful: a platform. And for those who learn how to use it correctly, it is one of the most reliable wealth engines ever built. In the succinct words of Thomas Edison. " There's a way to do it better—find it."

CHAPTER 2

INCOME IS NOT WEALTH: THE LIE I WAS TAUGHT, AND BELIEVED FOR TOO LONG

"Rich people acquire assets. The poor and middle class acquire liabilities that they think are assets."
– Robert Kiyosak

For much of my career, I truly believed that income was simply wealth delayed. I assumed that if I kept earning at a high level, stayed disciplined, and avoided stupidity, the math would eventually work in my favor. I didn't think of myself as financially naïve. In fact, I thought I was being prudent. I saved consistently. I funded retirement accounts. I avoided speculative nonsense. From the outside, my financial life looked responsible, even exemplary.

And yet, the longer I practiced, the more uneasy I became.

What I couldn't articulate at first—but eventually couldn't ignore—was that income felt busy but not durable. It created motion, not momentum. Every year I earned more, but every year the system required more from me in return. More work. More responsibility. More exposure. More dependency.

Income is seductive because it is visible. You see it on contracts, pay stubs, W-2s, and tax returns. You feel it when your lifestyle expands. Bigger house. Better cars. Private school tuition. Travel that feels "earned." But income has a hidden flaw: it is conditional. It exists only as long as you keep producing.

I didn't fully grasp that fragility until I started looking at where the money actually went.

Take taxes alone. For a high-earning professional, earned income is taxed first and hardest. Federal marginal tax rates reach 37%. Add state income tax—often 5% to 10% depending on where you live. Add Medicare tax at 2.9%, plus the additional 0.9% surtax at higher income levels. Add the Net Investment Income Tax of 3.8% once certain thresholds are crossed. Before you've saved a dollar, your income has already been reduced by 45% to 50% in many cases.

I remember running the numbers for the first time and realizing something unsettling: nearly half of what I earned never even made it into my hands. It was gone before I had any say in how it was used.

And taxes were only the beginning.

High income tends to attract fixed obligations. Mortgage payments expand. Property taxes increase. Insurance premiums rise—malpractice, umbrella, disability, life. Education costs climb, especially when private school or out-of-state college tuition enters the picture. These expenses don't flex downward easily. Once established, they harden.

I started noticing how many physicians around me were locked into financial structures that required constant income just to stand still. Miss a few months of earnings and the stress would surface immediately. That realization forced me to confront a difficult truth: high income did not equal financial safety. In many cases, it simply disguised how exposed people really were.

Wealth behaves differently.

Wealth is not dependent on your schedule. It doesn't require your physical presence. It doesn't care whether you worked sixty hours this week or took a month off. Wealth exists because something you own continues to function without you.

> "If you don't find a way to make money while you sleep, you will work until you die."
> – Warren Buffett

The data around this distinction is striking. Studies of household net worth consistently show that individuals who derive a meaningful portion of income from ownership—business equity, real assets, or scalable enterprises—accumulate wealth faster and with less volatility than those dependent primarily on wages or professional fees. The driver is not savings rate. It's leverage and tax treatment.

I became particularly aware of how the tax code treats effort versus ownership. Earned income is taxed annually, immediately, and at the highest rates. Asset income can often be deferred. Depreciation allows income to exist on paper while taxes are postponed or eliminated entirely. Capital gains are taxed at lower rates than ordinary income. Losses can offset gains. Timing can be controlled.

That contrast changes outcomes dramatically over time.

Consider this: a professional earning $600,000 in pure labor income might pay $270,000 to $300,000 annually in combined taxes. Over twenty years, that can easily exceed $5 million transferred to taxing authorities. Meanwhile, an individual earning a smaller amount of cash flow from owned assets may legally pay a fraction of that through depreciation, interest deductions, and strategic structuring. The difference isn't morality. It's math.

What troubled me was realizing how little control income offers. I didn't control reimbursement. I didn't control payer mix. I didn't control regulatory shifts, contract renewals, or administrative policy changes. I could work harder, but I couldn't negotiate from a position of strength unless I had alternatives.

That's when the idea of resilience started to matter more than earnings.

Financial resilience isn't about how much you make in a good year. It's about how you fare in a bad one. Data on high-income households shows that a surprising percentage lack meaningful liquidity. Even among earners above $300,000, a significant portion would struggle to maintain lifestyle for six to twelve months without active income. I found that alarming—not because people were irresponsible, but because income-dependent systems are inherently brittle.

Wealth absorbs shock. Income amplifies it.

This forced me to change the questions I asked myself. I stopped obsessing over marginal increases in compensation. A $50,000 raise felt far less interesting once I understood how little of it I would actually keep—and how dependent it made me on continued output. Instead, I started asking whether a decision increased my optionality. Whether it reduced dependency. Whether it created something that existed independently of me.

Medicine trains us to value effort. We are rewarded for showing up, staying late, taking call, pushing harder. That mindset is excellent for patient care. It is terrible for wealth creation. Effort scales linearly. Ownership does not.

I also began paying attention to how institutions think. Hospitals don't obsess over income. They obsess over assets, control, and repeatability. Insurers focus on risk pools and long-term margins. Investment firms care about scalability, exit multiples, and cash flow durability. None of them rely on personal labor. They rely on structure.

Physicians, ironically, sit at the center of this entire ecosystem. We generate the revenue that makes everything else possible. Yet most of us remain positioned at the most fragile point in the structure: highly paid, highly taxed, and highly dependent.

Even disciplined investing has limits when it is fueled solely by earned income. Retirement accounts are important, but they are constrained. Contribution limits cap how much can be deployed annually. Withdrawals are restricted by age. Market volatility introduces sequence risk. Future tax rates are unknown. These vehicles are passive by design. They rarely create meaningful optionality early in life.

What finally became clear to me is that income answers a very narrow question: What did I do this month? Wealth answers a broader one: What will still be here if I stop?

Once I understood that distinction, I couldn't unsee it. I noticed how often physicians solved the income problem brilliantly while never addressing the wealth problem at all. I noticed how many career decisions were driven by compensation alone, without regard for durability or control. I noticed how quickly high earners could become trapped by the very income they celebrated.

Income is necessary. It funds opportunity. It creates access. But it is not the destination.

Wealth is what remains when effort slows. It is what provides insulation against uncertainty. It is what allows you to negotiate from strength, to walk away when needed, to choose rather than react. That realization didn't make me work less hard. It made me far more intentional about what my work was building.

I stopped asking how much something paid. I started asking what it produced, what it protected, and what it could become over time.

That shift—quiet, internal, and uncomfortable at first—changed everything.

"Rich people acquire assets. The poor and middle class acquire liabilities that they think are assets."

– Robert Kiyosaki

CHAPTER 3

THE HEALTHCARE WEALTH STACK: WHERE I FINALLY SAW HOW MONEY REALLY MOVES

"You do not rise to the level of your goals. You fall to the level of your systems."
– James Clear

For a large part of my career, I believed money in healthcare followed a simple and almost honorable path: a patient needs care, I provide it, and compensation follows. That belief made perfect sense from the physician's chair. It also kept me blind to how healthcare actually functions as an economic system. The first time I forced myself to stop thinking like a clinician and start thinking like an owner, everything shifted. I realized money in healthcare doesn't move horizontally. It moves vertically. And each vertical layer captures a completely different share of value.

At the bottom of the healthcare wealth stack sits clinical labor. This is where I began, and where the overwhelming majority of physicians remain for their entire careers. Clinical work is indispensable, but financially constrained by design. Across multiple specialties, professional services typically operate at operating margins between 5% and 12% after staffing, billing costs, malpractice insurance, compliance infrastructure, and administrative overhead are fully loaded. In employed physician models, internal cost allocations can reduce the physician's effective retained margin to single digits, sometimes as low as 3–5% of the total revenue generated.

I remember the first time I saw a full revenue breakdown tied to my own work. For every dollar generated, only a small fraction was truly attributable to me after institutional costs were carved out. The rest flowed elsewhere—quietly, predictably, and permanently.

Above clinical labor sit facilities and ancillary services, and this is where the financial physics change. Ambulatory facilities routinely operate at EBITDA margins of 20–30% once stabilized. Independent laboratories that achieve sufficient test volume benefit from automation, batching, and centralized processing, allowing margins to exceed 25% and, in some cases, approach 35% when fixed costs are diluted across scale. Imaging centers follow a similar pattern. Once utilization thresholds are reached, MRI and CT operations can generate margins north of 30%, especially when equipment financing, depreciation schedules, and utilization rates are optimized. Pharmacies, while operating on thinner per-unit margins, benefit from predictable refill behavior, recurring revenue, and customer stickiness that produces stable, compounding cash flow year after year.

What struck me was not just the size of these margins, but their consistency. These businesses did not require heroic effort to outperform clinical labor financially. They required structure.

"Money is a terrible master but an excellent servant."
– P.T. Barnum

Then comes the layer most physicians never truly reach: ownership, consolidation, and control. This is where wealth accelerates dramatically. Single-location medical practices often transact at 3–5x EBITDA. Facilities with strong governance, diversified payor mix, and operational maturity trade higher. Multi-site platforms, management services organizations, and vertically integrated healthcare assets frequently command valuation multiples of 8–12x EBITDA, and in competitive markets, multiples can exceed that range entirely.

That multiple expansion is not theoretical. It is the engine of wealth creation in healthcare.

I remember running a simple comparison that permanently changed my thinking. A physician working full time for twenty or thirty years might generate millions in cumulative income, pay millions in taxes, and exit with a portfolio dependent on market performance. Meanwhile, a healthcare asset producing $3 million in annual EBITDA sold at a 10x multiple results in a $30 million valuation event in a single transaction. The difference was not intelligence, dedication, or clinical excellence. It was position in the stack.

Capital understands this hierarchy instinctively. Institutional investors do not analyze healthcare through effort or hours worked. They evaluate asset control, margin durability, contract stability, and exit optionality. This is why healthcare consistently ranks among the top destinations for private capital deployment. Fragmentation enables consolidation. Predictable utilization supports leverage. Regulatory complexity creates barriers to entry. Aging demographics ensure demand growth. These are structural advantages that capital seeks relentlessly.

I began noticing how reliably money flows uphill. Clinical labor generates revenue. Facilities and ancillaries multiply it. Ownership captures it. This isn't ideology—it's mechanics. The higher you move in the stack, the less your returns depend on personal effort and the more they depend on systems that operate continuously.

Another set of numbers shifted my perspective even further. Owned assets benefit from depreciation schedules that can shelter cash flow for years. Capital expenditures reduce taxable income while increasing enterprise value. Debt amortizes while equity appreciates. In contrast, clinical income resets every year and is taxed annually. Over a decade, these structural differences alone can create disparities measured in millions of dollars.

I also started paying attention to where real power sat. Many of the wealthiest people in healthcare were not the busiest or the most visible. They weren't on call. They weren't maximizing RVUs. They controlled facilities, management entities, or platforms that others depended on to function. They sat at the intersection of infrastructure and capital, letting volume and scale work on their behalf.

Once I understood the healthcare wealth stack clearly, confusion disappeared. I no longer wondered why some physicians worked relentlessly and still felt financially constrained, while others seemed to slow down and accelerate at the same time. They weren't gaming the system. They were positioned differently within it.

That realization was uncomfortable. It forced me to accept that excellence at the bottom of the stack does not grant automatic access to the top. Movement upward is intentional. It requires a shift in identity—from producer to owner, from participant to architect.

But once you see the stack for what it is, you stop chasing income blindly. You start thinking vertically. You ask where you sit, which layer you occupy, and which structures actually reward ownership rather than effort.

That was the moment healthcare stopped looking like a job to me and started looking like a system. And systems, once understood, can be navigated deliberately rather than endured passively.

"An investment in knowledge pays the best interest."
– Benjamin Franklin

CHAPTER 4

OWNERSHIP CHANGES EVERYTHING: THE MOMENT I STOPPED BEING THE PRODUCT

"You must gain control over your money or the lack of it will forever control you."
– Dave Ramsey

There was a very specific point in my career when I realized that no matter how skilled I was, no matter how hard I worked, and no matter how much revenue I personally generated, I was still fundamentally replaceable. That realization wasn't emotional. It wasn't philosophical. It was financial.

As long as I was paid only for what I personally did, I was the product. And products don't scale.

In professional medicine, compensation is still largely anchored to individual output. You are paid per procedure, per visit, per shift, or per unit of productivity. Even when compensation looks generous, it is bounded by time. A day still has twenty-four hours. A year still has a fixed number of working days. Once I internalized that reality, it became obvious that income growth eventually plateaus—sometimes early, sometimes late, but always permanently.

Ownership changes that equation entirely.

I started looking at wealth data outside medicine, and the pattern was unmistakable. According to longitudinal wealth studies, individuals with equity ownership in operating businesses experience compound net worth growth at rates significantly higher than wage-based professionals, even when annual cash income is lower. What matters is not how much comes in each year, but whether value accumulates independently of continued effort.

I paid close attention to balance sheets instead of paychecks.

One of the most striking differences I saw was how equity behaves over time. A business asset that grows revenue at even a modest 5–7% annually can double in value in a little over a decade—without the owner working harder. That same growth rate applied to personal income does not compound in the same way, because income is consumed and taxed annually. Equity compounds quietly in the background.

" Earn with your mind, not your time."
– Naval Ravikant

I also began studying transaction data. In healthcare acquisitions, assets with repeatable revenue, governance structure, and operational depth command premiums that have nothing to do with the founder's day-today involvement. Buyers pay for continuity. They pay for predictability. They pay for systems that survive personnel changes. None of those things apply to labor.

That was sobering.

Another set of numbers caught my attention: income concentration versus wealth concentration. High-earning professionals represent a relatively large share of top income brackets, but a much smaller share of top wealth brackets. The gap is filled almost entirely by owners—people who control enterprises, not hours. That distinction explained something I had observed anecdotally for years but never quantified.

Ownership also changes risk in ways most people misunderstand.

From the outside, ownership looks riskier than employment. In reality, dependence on a single paycheck is often far more fragile. Data on income interruption shows that professionals dependent on one employer or one revenue stream experience sharper financial stress during disruptions than those with diversified ownership interests. A business can lose one contract and survive. An individual losing a job absorbs the full impact immediately.

I also began to understand how ownership changes cash-flow timing. Employees receive income on a fixed schedule and pay taxes immediately. Owners decide when distributions occur. Owners choose whether profits are reinvested, held, or distributed. Owners can refinance assets, extract capital without selling, or defer liquidity entirely. Timing control alone can materially alter lifetime financial outcomes.

Then there is valuation—something physicians are almost never taught to think about.

Income has no multiple. It resets every year. Equity does. Businesses are valued on future cash flow, not past effort. A well-structured operating entity can increase in value even during periods when the owner is less active. That concept took me time to fully absorb, because it runs counter to how we are trained. In medicine, value is tied to presence. In ownership, value is tied to position.

What ownership ultimately gave me was leverage.

Leverage in negotiations. Leverage in career decisions. Leverage in how I allocated my time. When income is your only engine, every contract feels critical. Every call schedule feels personal. Every reimbursement change feels threatening. When ownership provides baseline security, decisions become strategic rather than reactive.

I noticed how my posture changed. I became more selective. More patient. Less pressured. I could afford to think long-term instead of chasing short-term certainty.

Perhaps the most underappreciated effect of ownership is psychological. When you stop being the product, your relationship with work changes. You stop equating self-worth with output. You stop confusing busyness with progress. You start evaluating decisions based on durability rather than immediacy.

There is an uncomfortable truth most professionals avoid: skills age, contracts expire, and institutions reorganize. No matter how good you are, labor is temporary. Ownership is what survives transitions.

Once I crossed that line—once I stopped being paid only for what I did and started being paid for what I owned—everything shifted. My tolerance for short-term discomfort increased. My dependence on any single institution disappeared. My thinking extended decades instead of quarters.

Ownership didn't make me work less. It made my work matter longer.

And once I understood that difference fully, there was no going back.

"It's not about ideas. It's about making ideas happen."
– Scott Belsky

CHAPTER 5

BEFORE YOU INVEST: ARMING YOURSELF FOR THE REAL GAME

"Give me six hours to chop down a tree and I will spend the first four sharpening the axe."
– Abraham Lincoln

Up to this point, I've focused on how I think about wealth—what actually creates it, what quietly destroys it, and why high income alone is never enough. That groundwork matters, because without it, everything that follows risks being misunderstood. I'm not interested in offering shortcuts or a menu of "things to buy." Wealth in healthcare doesn't come from copying someone else's deal. It comes from understanding the terrain.

That is what the next section of this book is about.

Before you ever decide what to invest in, you need to understand how the system works. Most failed investments in healthcare are not the result of bad intent or poor effort. They fail because the investor didn't understand the rules that govern money, valuation, and risk. I learned—sometimes the hard way—that knowledge is the real leverage.

The chapters that follow are about weapons, not targets.

Taxes determine how much of every dollar you actually keep. EBITDA determines how businesses are valued, not how hard you worked to build them. Regulatory frameworks—antitrust laws, Stark Law, anti-kickback statutes—define what is permissible long before a deal ever looks attractive. Ignore them, and no amount of upside will save you. Understand them, and entire categories of opportunity suddenly make sense.

I also want to demystify the formulas and mental models that serious investors use instinctively. How value is calculated. How risk is priced. How structure alters outcomes more than revenue ever will. These are not academic concepts. They are practical tools that change how you see every opportunity that comes across your desk.

I am deliberately not telling you what to invest in.

Instead, I'm giving you the knowledge to walk into any investment—inside or outside healthcare—with clarity, confidence, and control. The goal is not to follow someone else's path. The goal is to become dangerous enough to choose your own.

Once you are properly armed, the battlefield looks very different. As Benjamin Franklin said, " An investment in knowledge pays the best interest."

CHAPTER 6

BUSINESS TAX STRATEGIES

Render therefore unto Caesar the things which are Caesar's, and unto God the things that are God's.
—Jesus Christ

To succeed in business, the cardinal rule is not what you make, but what you get to keep. We are all aware of the dreadful overhead expenses that befall each business. These are moving targets that, to an extent, are controlled and placated by your business acumen. What is more complex and hard to navigate is the tax levied on your earnings. While it's a straightforward and manageable endeavor for the employed, it's a Medusa's head of biting exclusions and deductions for people owning multiple entities. To truly win the game of business, you must master this beast.

Death and Taxes: Death Remains Simple, But Tax Laws Are More Complex Than Ever

Our new Constitution is now established, everything seems to promise it will be durable; but, in this world, nothing is certain except death and taxes.
—Benjamin Franklin, in a 1789 letter to French Scientist Jean-Baptiste Le Roy a year after the US Constitution was ratified

They're both certain, as the saying goes, but while death remains the same, the living's tax laws are complex and ever-changing. Yet, if you understand them, you can utilize them properly and thereby help a business—yours—increase its profits.

Why, you miserable, cowardly, wretched little caterpillar! Don't you ever want to become a butterfly? Don't you want to spread your wings and flap your way to glory?
–Max Bialystock, from *The Producers*

Partnering with the tax code is not like tickling a dragon's tail. It can allow you to become that butterfly. You may eventually become a butterfly, but taking real advantage of the tax code shortens your time in the chrysalis. Admittedly, given the whirlwind changes in the tax code each year, it's a difficult task.

The complexities of tax law are increasing without bounds. They are so complex and multidimensional that only people who live, breathe, and eat each new tax law du jour can keep up. We call these people CPAs, or better, tax attorneys. Meanwhile, since you live, breathe, and eat what you do best, you are in a different position from the tax experts.

So, no, you can't know what they know. This brings me to the list of using tax laws to your business's advantage, beginning with the obvious first.

What everyone overlooks in the drumbeats of "Corporate America is Evil" is that you are legally and ethically allowed to maximize your tax deductions to the point where a highly complex, multilayered business may pay practically no federal taxes. There is much uproar across all political fronts about that, but has anyone ever wondered about that one group that never raises an issue with it that is the IRS? How many IRS agents do you ever see picketing the Microsoft office or the Apple headquarters?

None. And the reason is simple. It's your prerogative to avail of these deductions. A tax deduction is like the reclining seat on a plane. You might piss someone off behind you but damn it, it is your seat, and you can do with it what you want.

Below is a list of ways businesses can use tax laws to their advantage. If you want, copy-and-paste this list onto a memo to the person you hire in step one and do what they say.

Alternatively, I recommend taking each subsequent step, two through ten, as a learning experience. You don't have to learn as much as the expert, but it is wise to understand what applies to just you and your business. You may not be in pork bellies, so you don't have to know about them. But anything you learn about your own business is worth the effort.

The list—that is, for *this* year:

1. Hire a tax expert, or at the very least, consult with a tax professional frequently.

2. Keep accurate records.

3. Maximize deductions.

4. Utilize tax credits.

5. Defer income.

6. Plan for retirement.

7. Structure the business correctly.

8. Take advantage of tax-free investments.

9. Review international tax laws.

10. Consider the impact of state taxes.

Hire a Tax Expert

The hardest thing in the world to understand is the income tax.
—Albert Einstein

If you can't keep up with the profuse tax code tomes being generated all the time, let them do the keeping up. Tax laws are complex, and businesses should seek professional advice on how best to use them. Every time. Without exception. Otherwise, you leave money on the table.

A tax professional can help your business develop a tax strategy while ensuring that you comply with all relevant laws.

Keep Accurate Records

Americans spend three billion hours per year filling out tax forms and keeping tax records.

Keep accurate records. Keeping accurate and detailed records of all business transactions is essential for tax purposes and will make it easier for your business to claim deductions and credits and ensure it can comply with tax laws.

Today's world of block copy-and-pasting, scanning, and collating emails by the labels you create makes prepping for your returns easy. However, if your documentation is a heap of scraps in open boxes, you'll take months to prepare instead of just a day. Maybe even the lion's share of those three billion hours.

You really need to be on top of what you own, and you've got to be on top of your recordkeeping. Imagine one day if a major bank is taken down and the records are gone.
—Ross Perot, Jr.

Ross Perot, Jr. championed himself as a simple, direct man. With all due respect to Mr. Perot, get a scanner and establish a tree of truncated PDFs that can be backed up. Put your eggs in one basket, then duplicate those baskets among several basket depositories—on an external drive, Dropbox, and other archival devices.

Another way is to email yourself receipts and payments. Most are available via email as an option, and you can send it to yourself with something pertinent in the subject line, like "Receipts," "Entertainment," "Charity Donation," "Durable Equipment," and so on. You can make additional email labels for the year, take the emails with the respective subjects, and label them with multiple tags.

For example, you bought some durable equipment for which you're entitled to a tax credit. You can assign the email of the receipt to the labels "2023," "Durable Equipment," "Tax Credits," "Business Deductible," and so on. Think of putting "Deductible" in the search field of your email service and seeing hundreds of emails with the attachments.

One thing for which computers are great is categorizing, cross-categorizing, subcategorizing, duplicate categorizing, and combining categories. Google, Apple, or other prominent email players are less likely to crash than your external drive or the backup startup you use.

Besides keeping accurate records, add to them daily. Don't be the guy cramming for finals as April 15 looms; you won't get to it all, and when the deadlines strike, something forgotten will be left on the proverbial table, wasted.

Maximize Deductions

Few of us ever test our powers of deduction, except when filling out an income tax form.
—Laurence J. Peter, best known for the Peter Principle, which centered on competency limits and promotions

Tax deductions reduce a business's taxable income and, thus, its tax liability. Companies should take advantage of all available deductions for business expenses, equipment, and charitable contributions. Once you subtract all business costs, including depreciation, you get down to the real result—your take-home pay (aka, your net income). Putting as much distance between your gross and your net would be best.

As ominous as the tax system is, remember that it is actually business-friendly. Make friends with it and take advantage of all the deductions the government allows, for they are permitted solely to make your business successful. Those deductions are out there, trust me. An unsuccessful business can't pay taxes, as Max Bialystock and Leo Bloom demonstrated so well in *The Producers*.

A few examples of business tax deductions are:

1. **Business Expenses:** Businesses can deduct various expenses, such as rent, utilities, office supplies, and advertising.

2. **Employee Expenses**: Businesses can deduct the cost of benefits, such as retirement plans, health insurance, and training programs for employees.

3. **Equipment and Vehicle Expenses**: Businesses can deduct the cost of equipment, such as computers and machinery, and the cost of maintaining and operating vehicles and other durable goods used for business purposes.

4. **Home Office Expenses**: Business owners who use a part of their home for business purposes can deduct a portion of their property taxes, mortgage interest, insurance, and utilities—maintenance, too, with your accountant's sanction. Use your tape measure and see what percentage of your home your office is. This has become very important lately with the remote work revolution the pandemic has engendered.

5. **Travel and Entertainment Expenses**: Businesses can deduct travel and entertainment expenses, such as meals, lodging, transportation, and event tickets, as long as they can be directly related to the business and are not considered lavish or extravagant. Volume determines lavishness and extravagance. Keeping it down lowers the red flag.

6. **Charitable Contributions**: Businesses can deduct the cost of charitable contributions, such as donations by the company, to nonprofit organizations that comply with specific tax laws. However, you can personally benefit from a contribution to a 501(c) (3) organization (but not a 501 [c]).

7. **Research and Development Costs**: Businesses can deduct the cost of researching and developing new products, processes, or software as long as they are directly related to the business and comply with specific tax laws.

8. **Depreciation**: Businesses can also deduct the cost of assets, such as buildings and equipment, over a period of time through depreciation.

9. **Health Savings Account Contributions**: If the business has a high-deductible health plan, it can set up a health savings account (HSA) and deduct contributions to the account made by the company. There are established limits, so it helps to know what they are and reach them each year.

10. **Bad Debt**: If a business has made a loan or extended credit to a customer and cannot collect, the business may be able to deduct that amount.

These examples are not the complete list and are subject to change over time. Tax laws and regulations are subject to change, and consulting with a tax professional is recommended to confirm the deductions that apply to your business.

Utilize Tax Credits

Taxes are what we pay for civilized society.
—Oliver Wendell Holmes, Jr., US Supreme Court Justice

Ah, yes, but:

A government that robs Peter to pay Paul can always rely on the support of Paul.
—George Bernard Shaw

Tax credits are more valuable than deductions because they directly lower the taxes a business owes. That is, take the net income of the above paragraphs, come up with your true taxable income, then happily get out an eraser.

Various tax credits, such as those for hiring employees from certain groups, making energy-efficient improvements, and investing in research and development, are available. Remember that besides having a business-friendly tax code (so you can make more and pay more taxes), the government also uses that same tax code to push political, social, and even ecological agendas.

But agendas change. If you're wavering on making a green investment in your business, for example, all it takes is the next midterm election to make that disappear. Thus, besides knowing how you'll keep more of your money by getting that agenda-friendly and agenda-sanctioned credit now, you also must figure out how much *not* doing this may cost you next year when it's no longer available.

Defer Income

Procrastination is something best put off until tomorrow.
—Politician Gerald Vaughan

By deferring income to a future tax year, a business can reduce its current year's tax liability until the rate may be lower. It will never be lower because tax rates go down, but it will be lower when you take the income and pay lower taxes—for example, when you retire.

Interest, dividends, or capital gains won't count until you cash in. Deferring income means delaying cashing in. This can be done by postponing billings or collections or by accelerating expenses. A retirement vehicle or an IRA are excellent examples. (However, you still have to pay Medicare and Social Security taxes.)

Plan for Retirement

> A cardinal rule in budgeting and saving is to pay yourself first. Once your paycheck hits your account, wisdom has it that you should move some amount to savings even before you pay the bills.
> —American businessman John Rampton

Speaking of retirement vehicles, contributions to retirement plans such as a 401(k) or SEP IRA can provide significant tax savings. This idea is part of the deferred income idea, since not only do retirement contributions reduce a business's taxable income, but income earned in the plan grows tax-free until withdrawn. Or, as I said, until you "cash in."

Structure Your Business Correctly

> In business, organization is an absolute necessity, not an alternative.
> —Financial radio personality Larry Burkett

The type of business entity a business chooses can significantly impact its taxes. For example, an S corporation can provide personal asset protection and pass-through taxation, while a C corporation can offer lower tax rates on the first $75,000 of income.

An LLC may give you the best of all worlds since they are the "orphans" of the tax code, in that they don't have their own federal tax classification. They can adopt the tax status of sole proprietorships, partnerships, or S or C corporations.

This topic belongs to the first: *hire a tax expert.*

Take Advantage of Tax-Free Investments

The best things in life are tax-free.
—Author Joseph Bonkowski

Certain investments, such as municipal bonds, may be tax-free at the federal level. Businesses should consider these types of investments as a way to save on taxes. They are designed to encourage investing in infrastructures and other things generally good for society.

Your country, state, or municipality rewards you by letting you reap your due profits without tax liabilities.

Mind International Tax Laws

Review international tax laws. Many businesses have a global presence and must be aware of international tax laws. Again, *hire a tax expert.*

Tax treaties and other agreements can help businesses save on taxes by avoiding double taxation and other overlapping border-crossing arithmetic. Take advantage of these opportunities.

However, such arrangements may be a double-edged sword. Borders mean politics. How will your arrangement change when a crazy man starts a war, and you have to suffer the sanctions that result?

Remember the State You're In

> Hawaii is the most unique state in the country. No other states are especially similar to it. In fact, for most states, Hawaii is their least similar state. This is unsurprising since the distance between Hawaii and the other states is vast.
> –State Similarity Index

Consider the impact of state taxes. They can vary widely, and businesses should consider state taxes' impact when deciding where to locate or expand their operations. Where a company is anchored legally vs. where it operates are two different things. There may be more to minding your state than just the taxes it wants you to pay. A state is no different from a mini-federal government. You can get in trouble with one without getting in trouble with the other, but any trouble is too much. Avoid all trouble: remember your lil ol' state and its expectations of you.

In conclusion, using tax laws to increase business profits requires a comprehensive understanding of those laws and regulations that apply to the business. Businesses should take the time to research and plan accordingly. If you can't, hire a professional. Even if you can, hire a professional anyway.

Businesses can reduce their tax liability by taking advantage of deductions, credits, and other opportunities and properly structuring their operations. Additionally, keeping accurate records and consulting with that tax professional can help businesses make the most of the tax laws and increase their profits.

Taxation is the price which civilized communities pay for the opportunity of remaining civilized.
–Harvard history professor Albert Bushnell Hart

The conundrum of death and taxes—you should live rich, not die rich.

Your government wants you to succeed, but not because it is your friend or wants rainbows and pixie dust in your life. It wants you to succeed so you can pay more taxes. But taxes are good—they educate your children, care for older people, allow us to travel on roadways, and run your country. Most of the time—and I reserve the right to rescind this statement—the tax code stands to deliver a win-win scenario. If you don't meet it halfway by taking advantage of what it has to offer, it's a win-lose. Don't be a loser. Don't be a Peter!

While I don't profess to be a tax professional, here is a comprehensive checklist of deductions every business should take to maximize profits. A penny saved is a penny earned. And pennies add up.

1. Home office expenses

2. Business travel expenses

3. Meals and entertainment expenses

4. Car and truck expenses

5. Business insurance premiums

6. Interest on business loans and credit cards
7. Legal and professional fees
8. Rent or lease of business property
9. Depreciation on business property and equipment
10. Employee wages and salaries
11. Employee benefits, such as health insurance and retirement plans
12. Self-employed health insurance deduction
13. Advertising and promotion expenses
14. Business gifts to clients and employees
15. Charitable contributions made by the business
16. Conferences and trade show attendance
17. Online and offline subscriptions related to business
18. Domain registration and website hosting
19. Business licenses and permits
20. Bank fees and merchant account fees
21. Computer hardware and software expenses
22. Training and education expenses for employees

23. Travel and accommodation expenses for training
24. Telephone and internet expenses
25. Repair and maintenance expenses for business property and equipment
26. Office supplies and stationery expenses
27. Postage and shipping expenses
28. Shipping supplies expenses
29. Cleaning and janitorial expenses
30. Utility expenses
31. Printing and copying expenses
32. Furniture and fixture expenses
33. Business books and magazines
34. Donations to local charities and nonprofits
35. Royalties and licensing fees
36. Property taxes on business property
37. Investment fees and expenses
38. Research and development expenses
39. Meals and lodging expenses for business conferences

40. Moving expenses for the business
41. Job search expenses for hiring employees
42. Credit monitoring and identity theft protection for the business
43. Uniforms and protective clothing expenses
44. Damaged or stolen goods and property expenses
45. Bad debts expenses
46. Credit card processing fees
47. Collection agency fees
48. Travel expenses for sales reps
49. Subcontractor expenses
50. Bankruptcy expenses
51. Business membership fees
52. Product development expenses
53. Equipment rentals
54. Teleconferencing and video conferencing expenses
55. Audio and video equipment expenses
56. Leasehold improvements

57. Employee discounts
58. Rent for storage facilities
59. Insurance for equipment and inventory
60. Property insurance premiums
61. Business equipment repair and maintenance expenses
62. Licensing and certification fees
63. Hiring expenses such as recruiter fees
64. Equipment leasing expenses
65. Software licensing expenses
66. Meal and lodging expenses for overnight business trips
67. Parking expenses for business travel
68. Translation and interpretation expenses
69. Consulting and advisory fees
70. Temporary help expenses
71. Payroll service expenses
72. Filing and processing fees for business documents
73. Postage and courier expenses for delivering documents

74. Document destruction and shredding expenses
75. Patent and trademark registration fees
76. Business tax preparation expenses
77. Software development expenses
78. Social media advertising expenses
79. Political contributions made by the business
80. Cable and satellite TV expenses
81. Annual meeting expenses
82. Employee wellness program expenses
83. Disaster recovery expenses
84. Data backup expenses
85. Business license fees
86. Business formation expenses
87. Interest on business credit lines
88. Safety equipment expenses
89. Business appraisal fees
90. Expense reimbursement for employees

91. Workers' compensation insurance premiums
92. Employee transportation expenses
93. Employee recruitment advertising expenses
94. Employee background check expenses
95. Costs from business continuity plan development
96. Online advertising expenses
97. Event and exhibition expenses
98. Captive insurance (more on this later)
99. Continued education expenses while overseas
100. Travel expenses between businesses

The Captive Insurance Company.

Honorable mention should be made here of a rather advanced way of tax management for businesses that own and face multiple layers of financial exposure and risk: The Captive Insurance company. A captive insurance company is a subsidiary that helps businesses manage risk by owning their own insurance. It allows tailored coverage, improved control, and cost-effective protection. Furthermore, it offers potential tax advantages through strategic tax planning, resulting in savings on federal taxes.

To delve a little deeper into the topic, a captive insurance company is an insurance company that is set up for the benefit and at the behest of an affiliated entity. There are many different types of captive insurance companies from a pure/stand-alone captive, a cell captive, and a group captive. The pure/stand-along captive is one where there is no core and separate entities underneath the core. It typically has higher regulatory fees, higher capitalization requirements, etc. as it literally stands on its own. The cell captive is one where there is a core entity then separate "cells" are segregated off from the core. These cells typically have lower regulatory fees and minimum capital requirements because they are sharing those at the core level. Finally, a group captive is one where typically a group of insureds from either a common industry (i.e. Doctors, attorneys, CPAs, home builders, etc.) will start a captive insurance company together to buy a certain coverage as a group, typically to get a "group" discount on the coverage being purchased.

Traditional captive insurance companies write property and casualty ("P&C") risks. These are over 3,000 P&C risks that are accepted by the National Association of Insurance Commissioners ("NAIC"). These risks can range from writing a business's worker's compensation, auto, property, and umbrella, to more specific coverage lines such as cyber, Directors and Officers ("D&O"), administrative action/governmental intervention, and crime policies. If large enough, and the business has the risk appetite to do so, the business can also choose to write a portion, or even all of their employees' health care coverage into a captive insurance company.

Finally, in terms of the taxation of captive insurance companies, taxes should never be the primary driver of doing a captive insurance company so please be careful how you look at the tax side of a captive insurance company. I asked Jeff Andrews, Esquire from Ryan Captive, LLC, to opine on the tax aspect of Captive Insurance Companies. Here is his summary: There are three ways that they can be taxed. The first is simply as a corporation, where there is no election being made to be taxed as an insurance company. The captive will run as any other business and will be taxed at C-Corp tax rates (21% currently) under tax form 1120. The second is as an insurance company under code section 831(a). Under this election, the captive insurance company is still taxed on its net income at

C-Corp tax rates, but are able to take a current year deduction for future claim reserves typically referred to as Outstanding Loss Reserve ("OSLR") or Incurred But Not Reported ("IBNR") if their actuary determines that they have these reserves in the lines of coverage that they are writing. The final way of taxing a captive is under code section 831(b). This is where if your premium is under $2.65MM (changes each year based on inflation), your captive can elected to be taxed on its investment income only. In other words, a medium or large sized business can put upwards of tax deductible 2 million US dollars yearly into their own captive company. At the top marginal federal tax rate of 40%, that's close to a million dollars in tax savings every year.

CHAPTER 7

EBITDA

" Profit is not something to add on at the end. It is something to plan for in the beginning."
—Jim Rohn

The first step you will encounter when buying/investing into a business is to know what its true worth is. That worth is the biggest bone of contention between the buyer and the seller. Mastering that worth will be the base pillar of your future in that entity. If you buy high, it will take you years to break even. That's money lost. And money lost is time wasted. Shorten the length of that wastage by learning the basic principles of purchase and valuation.

So You Want to *Buy* a Company…

It's far better to buy a wonderful company at a fair price than a fair company at a wonderful price.
—CEO, Berkshire Hathaway, Warren Buffett

So You Want to *Sell* a Company...

Nobody likes to be sold to, but everyone likes to buy.
—Teacher Earl Taylor

Introduction: Buying or Selling—Where Do You Start?

To the making and selling of things, there is no end...Man, it occurs to me, is a joyful, buying-and-selling piece of work... Consumerism is what we are. It is, in a sense, a holy impulse. A human being is someone who joyfully goes in pursuit of things, brings them home, then immediately starts planning how to get more.
—Author George Saunders

The first chapters of my book emphasized the motif of being ambitious: "going for it," and "nothing ventured, nothing gained." But imbued within all these affirmations is the idea that you have to be smart about it.

You cannot just saunter into the business world willy-nilly, throw your money down, and hope the dice come up with a winner. That's a sucker bet. Such are the people for whom casinos stay open all day and all night and, as showman P. T. Barnum rightly argued, "There's one born every minute."

True, gambling is any investment in which the outcome is uncertain, but the wise business investor is a gambler who substitutes wisdom and insight for blind luck. In casinos, the odds are stacked in the house's favor. Someone wins—usually the house; someone loses—usually you.

In business investing and the buying and selling of companies, however, the best results come when everyone wins. No suckers on both sides means it's a good deal. Selling or buying your company at a fair price, as Mr. Buffet claims, is wonderful. Live your life that way, and you won't leave a trail of enemies. Remember, the one with the fewest enemies has the most friends—friends when in need will be friends, indeed.

Who Says What's Fair? GAAP Earnings?

Buying and selling a business isn't just about the pitch. The pitch is salesmanship, which can vary from factual to criminally fabricated. So, how's one to know? What's a smart fella to use to vet a deal?

There has to be some benchmark for measuring the value of a business which can be used to establish its worth—for selling it, or, alternatively, for buying it.

On an official level, there are generally accepted accounting principles (GAAP) which are accounting standards created and administered by the Financial Accounting Standards Board (FASB) and governed by the US Securities and Exchange Commission (SEC).

GAAP is an industry standard that determines how information is presented to shareholders in an audited report and what must be disclosed in a business's financial statements. It is also accepted as the legitimate methodology for private companies in financial audits. If you're buying or selling a business, GAAP will be there.

Non-GAAP: The Rest of the Story

Things change. In selling your business or buying someone else's, you want to know the present situation and not necessarily rely on just the ugly caterpillars from the beginning. Does GAAP allow that? GAAP was originally designed to do just that. So, if you use GAAP, can you lose? Well...

It's a lot like selling your house you've lived in for a long time. The government wants in on the deal and needs to know what you paid and how much you sold it for. Hopefully, of course, that represents a profit. Thus, your profit can be taxed accordingly.

However, is it all profit? You had to replace all the toilets when you moved in. The pipes were lead, so you had to change them all out. The electrical system had to be brought up to code.

You added a swimming pool, a hot tub, and a cabana. The roof leaked, and you had a new one put on before you moved in. Suddenly, the profit you're taxed on has shrunk considerably.

But the buyer you're selling your house to doesn't care about any of that. The IRS did, but not your homebuyer. They only want to pay fair market value (or less!).

GAAP is the company you paid for and for which you paid many nonrecurring expenses, including the ugly caterpillars. Hopefully, you've put on your last new roof, but your prospective buyer doesn't care about your investment in your roof or your move-in (start-up) costs. The buyer just wants to pay a fair price.

Yet, if your buyer goes to the courthouse and finds you spent $400,000 less than what you're asking now, just a year later, you'll suffer their expected resentment due to the similar way GAAP can mislead a purchaser. While you two fight over how much you paid vs. how much you put into it to justify your asking price, you're both playing fools to its fair market value: that will determine what you sell it for, what it's bought for, and what it's worth.

Fair market worth is the present and the future, not the past. It is reality. GAAP alone isn't reality.

Enter capitalism, because a fair price will use other accounting methods consistent with the market and the fair market prices it creates. GAAP is not reality, but it's a good start.

Reality is frequently inaccurate.
—Author Douglas Adams

To determine reality, you have to (respectfully) circumvent the GAAP story—but not disregard it, because it's still important. However, put it in the footnotes of the generally unaccepted accounting principles, of which one is EBITDA.

EBITDA footnotes what should *not* be included in the final worth of something. It is the proverbial fine print that eliminates unfair metrics that would falsely value or devalue your house—or a company. This is because what's done is done, and the future is just as much a part of a business as its past—in fact, even more so.

EBITDA: The Fine Print

EBITDA is a measure of a company's operating performance
and is often used as a proxy for cash flow.
–Investopedia

EBITDA stands for Earnings Before Interest, Taxes, Depreciation, and Amortization.

When a business is being bought or sold, EBITDA is a clever way to evaluate the company's financial functioning and determine its value. Unlike GAAP, it is more indicative of the worth of a business to the prospective buyer because it eliminates the nonrecurring costs which erode true worth. The financial metric is commonly used to evaluate a company's ability to generate cash flow, financial performance, and profitability. It is the present. GAAP includes the past. For the future, you need both.

Performance, profitability, and cash stream are important in determining a business's value.

Since EBITDA is a non-GAAP metric, it won't be affected by a company's accounting methods, making it an objective measure of a company's financial performance. In other words, it "explains" what really happened.

EBITDA is calculated, as implied by its very name, by taking a company's operating income and adding back in depreciation, amortization, and other noncash charges, thereby enabling it to measure profitability and ability to generate cash flow.

But, Then, Is EBITDA Reality?

No, we're not there yet.

For example, EBITDA does not consider a company's tax liability, which can also significantly impact a company's financial performance. What to do?

Ah, but there's EBITDA's big brother, the multiple of EBITDA.

The multiple of EBITDA is used to establish the purchase price of a company. The protocol is to divide the purchase price of a company by its EBITDA. Since the purchase price has already dealt with such things as tax liability, then it's on the buyer or seller to judge whether or not its multiple of EBITDA is valid.

Purchase Price , EBITDA = Multiple of EBITDA

For instance, if a company has an EBITDA of $1 million and is sold for $10 million, its multiple of EBITDA is ten. This multiple compares different companies' values and determines if a company is overvalued or undervalued.

In the macrocosm of healthcare businesses, it behooves a savvy investor to know the ballpark multiples of EBITDA that different types of medical entities trade for. Principles of economics dictate that a business is a fair sell at three times the net earnings from the past year. That's an oversimplification because there is much more that goes into a purchase than last year's earnings (strength of the company, history of earnings, etc.), but in general, that number is what a fair price for a typical business is considered to be. Not so much on healthcare. While a retiring general practitioner's business may be scavenged for three times its net earnings, entities like ambulatory surgery centers command much higher numbers, frequently twelve to sixteen times EBITDA. More on this later.

When buying a business, the multiple of EBITDA is essential because a higher multiple of EBITDA indicates that the business is more valuable and may be worth paying a higher price for. Or so the asking price suggests.

Consider a multiple of EBITDA of ten and another of fifty. The one with fifty indicates a company five times more profitable, all things being equal, than the one with ten.

But we still aren't living reality all the way.

Then, is Multiple of EBITDA Reality?

Not so fast.

It's still pertinent to consider other factors like the industry the business is in, the company's growth potential, and the company's prospects. No multiple of EBITDA is valid if you're investing in television sets that aren't flatscreen, in horse-and-buggy vehicles, or in rotary telephones.

> The multiple of EBITDA is just one of many factors to consider when valuing a business. It's important also to consider the company's growth prospects, industry trends, and future prospects.
> –William G. Ferguson, Managing Director of Clearview Capital

The multiple of EBITDA is the buyer's toy. When a business is being sold, the seller will often provide EBITDA information as part of the process. The buyer will typically use EBITDA information to calculate a multiple of EBITDA, which is used to determine the value of the business. That buyer will always prefer the one with fifty over the one with ten. Bigger is a better value—or at least a fairer one.

When selling a business, the seller must also consider the multiple of EBITDA. A higher multiple of EBITDA indicates that the business is more valuable, has a great future, will become more valuable, and thus may be able to command a higher price. The seller is thus better served by focusing on increasing the EBITDA of the business because that will also increase the multiple of EBITDA and hence the selling price.

> The key to selling a business at a high multiple of EBITDA is to focus on increasing the EBITDA of the business.
> —John Warrillow, author of *Built to Sell*

For instance, if a company has an EBITDA of $1 million and the buyer is willing to pay a multiple of eight times EBITDA, the company's value would be $8 million. This multiple, however, can be adjusted based on factors such as the company's industry, growth prospects, and level of debt. Plus, some intangibles may figure into the company's future, such as its "sexiness."

Like tax liability, however, a similar limitation of EBITDA is that it does not include a company's debt. A company with considerable debt may have a lower EBITDA multiple than a company with a lower level of debt, even if the two companies have similar EBITDA levels. A company can suffer a lower EBITDA because of the higher interest expense on such debt.

Multiple EBITDA formulas also can vary greatly depending on the industry. Different industries have different average multiples of EBITDA, so it's important to consider the entire industry when determining the value of a business. As has been said, high-growth industries will generate a higher multiple of EBITDA. Again, think of non-flatscreen TVs, whose growth is DOA.

With apologies to Mr. Stromberg, I think he just defined "sexiness."

Conclusion

In conclusion, **EBITDA** (Earnings Before Interest, Taxes, Depreciation, and Amortization) is a commonly used financial metric to evaluate a company's financial performance and help determine its value. Therefore, it is a critical metric when buying and selling a business.

The **multiple of EBITDA** is used to determine a company's value and compare the value of different companies, because it considers things like tax liability, debt levels, capital expenditures, industry health, growth potential, and—most importantly—the future. (Where do you want to be five years from now? Not here! You want to be there!)

So, when *buying* a business, the multiple of EBITDA is an important factor to consider, along with other factors such as the aforementioned industry, growth potential, and prospects.

And when *selling* a business, the multiple of EBITDA is also an important factor to consider, meaning the seller is best served by increasing the EBITDA of the business to increase the multiple and, hence, the selling price.

GAAP is necessary because it's based on law. But to get the real story, you need the company's EBITDA, and if you want the rest of the story, you will live and die by the multiple of EBITDA.

CHAPTER 8

STARK LAWS

Justice is the constant and perpetual will to
render to each one his due.
—Ulpian

To do something right, you must know where you go wrong with it first. A brief introduction to the Stark laws will show healthcare investors what is genuinely one of the biggest Medusa heads waiting for them through the labyrinth of healthcare businesses. A pit that, just like the seductive presence of the goddess herself, lures you in with its promises of ever-multiplying profits with just a tad bit of foul play that seems almost too innocuous to be considered illegal. And yet, it is.

Introduction: Stark—Where Do We Even Start?

Well, as they say, it's complicated.

The Stark law (aka the Physician Self-Referral law) is a federal law prohibiting physicians from making referrals for certain services to the ones rendering those services (or their immediate family members) who stand to profit from the referrals. The law was passed in 1989 and was intended to prevent conflicts of interest and financial gain in the healthcare industry. It's a good thing—kind of.

The law applies to physicians participating in Medicare and Medicaid programs, since Americans should expect transparency in how their healthcare dollars are spent.

In 2021, the USA spent an estimated $12,318 per person on healthcare, $1,000 of which was on administrative costs alone. This is more than any other developed country on Earth and represents almost a fifth of our total gross domestic product (GDP). According to the Centers for Medicare and Medicaid Services, Medicare and Medicaid account for 37 percent of our national health expenditure.

Start With Stark

US Congressman Pete Stark initially introduced his (and twenty others') "Ethics in Patient Referrals Act," which died without a vote being called. However, versions of it were introduced as other provisions in several Omnibus Budget Reconciliation Acts in 1989 and 1993, commonly referred to as Stark I and II, respectively. Since then, this far-flung diaspora of provisions has been tweaked, added to, and revised, and the process continues. After final rules, interim final rules, and new final rules, we're up to Stark III.

> Those complications were added by high-priced lawyers who tried to build loopholes for their clients. The original law was pretty simple. It says anyone who takes a bribe, a split, a commission, or a kickback in exchange for referring services gets five years or a fifty-thousand-dollar fine.
>
> —Former US Representative Pete Stark, in 2013, on why he would favor repealing the Stark laws

Many of its definitions and descriptions regarding prohibited arrangements aren't relevant to the practice of medicine or even to Medicare reimbursement protocols. The conflated jargon has created difficulty, if not the unlikelihood, for physicians to understand the rules they must follow to avoid stiff fines and even incarceration.

Like most government oversight, such volumes of bureaucracy results are burdensome at best, only to not miss that one physician doing "bad" things. Thus, the irony is that the irrelevance of much of it seems a lot like a test ordered, which may yield many false positives just to avoid the false negatives. In medicine, that's just a poor quality test that would be rejected for reimbursement due to not passing muster in our evidence-based world; in government, it's part of the "gotcha" mentality that thrills regulators and even prosecutors.

The original assumption that inspired the Stark law, i.e., physician investments and ownership lead to dishonest profiteering, has never been realized. Additionally, other laws have been added to prevent bad actors from being tempted. The Medicare Anti-Kickback Statute would prohibit even getting a pair of Knicks tickets for referrals (the Anti-"Knickback" Statute?), the Medical Ethics Codes, and State Board regulatory oversight that circles their prey when temptation leads to engagement.

The Stark laws and the Medicare Anti-Kickback Statute differ; the former calls for civil penalties and fines, and the latter has criminal implications in fines and imprisonment. The former applies only to physician referrals to Medicare/Medicaid; the latter is broader in scope, i.e., anyone engaging in business with a federal healthcare program.

The benefits this law potentially provides are now outweighed by innovation, patient satisfaction and convenience, and benefits that can be given without it.

When a physician gets a great idea—the kind of ambition and initiative this book is about—there must be a sensibility in the sort of things that Stark is about. The paradox is that physicians don't understand it, but it's not because they're dumb; it may be because the entire Stark-verse has become so unwieldy as to be a dumb way to prohibit, as Pete Stark mentioned, "a bribe or a split or a commission or a kickback in exchange for referring services."

Even when a physician has the foresight to hire an attorney with expertise in these areas, it is common for that attorney to ask for clarification from the Inspector General's office before giving their blessing to a new venture.

One must memorize where they apply to summarize and understand the Stark laws. In healthcare, they apply to Designated Health Services (DHS).

These include:

1. clinical laboratory services
2. physical therapy services
3. occupational therapy services
4. outpatient speech-language pathology services
5. radiology and certain other imaging services
6. radiation therapy services and supplies
7. durable medical equipment and supplies
8. parenteral and enteral nutrients, equipment, and supplies

9. prosthetics, orthotics, and prosthetic devices and supplies
10. home health services
11. outpatient prescription drugs
12. inpatient and outpatient hospital services

The law also applies to any other item or service determined by the Secretary of Health and Human Services to be a DHS, which is continually growing.

Allow me to propound on this further.

Here are five healthcare entities included in the Stark prohibitions:

1. **Physician-Owned Hospitals**: The Stark law prohibits referring Medicare/Medicaid patients to hospitals where they or their immediate family members have a financial interest. This is designed to prevent you from putting your children or wife as owners to sidestep the stink test. (As per Stark, that still stinks.)

   Physician-owned hospitals are typically owned by a group of physicians who have invested in the hospital's ownership. As with the other healthcare applications below, the law prevents you from making referrals based on financial gain instead of what's best for the patient. (Maybe your patient doesn't have to stay in your physician-owned hospital for five days after a laparoscopy!)

2. **Imaging Services**: MRIs, CT scans, and X-rays. If a physician has a financial interest in an imaging center, they cannot refer Medicare/Medicaid patients to that center for imaging services.

This applies even if the physician is not personally involved in the imaging center's ownership but gains in other ways from that referral. (Maybe that CT scan for a cold is overkill?)

3. **Laboratory Services**: Services such as blood tests and urinalysis. If you're a physician with a financial interest in a laboratory, you cannot refer Medicare/Medicaid patients to that laboratory for testing. Again, this includes situations where the physician is not personally involved in the laboratory's ownership but gains in other ways, like selling phlebotomy equipment to the lab.

4. **Rehabilitation Services**: Physical therapy, occupational, and other ancillary therapies.

5. **Home Health Services**: Home health nursing and itinerant therapy services are also included.

Stark laws apply to referrals to entities that any number of your relatives may own, either partially or wholly. Just who are these family members who would disqualify you from referring to entities owned by them? It's actually a whole lot of people because, according to Stark, "immediate family" encompasses an extensive group of people: your spouse; your birth or adoptive parent, child, or sibling; your stepparent, stepchild, or stepsiblings; all of your in-laws; and your grandparents or grandchildren, or their spouses. ("My cousin, Vinny," is still under advisement.)

Designated Health Services (DHS): The Exceptions

Ignorance of the law is no excuse.
—Thomas Jefferson

The biggest problem with the Stark laws is not that they make it difficult, if not impossible, to make a living as a physician. You still can. You just have to work within the system.

No, the real problem with the Stark laws is that a physician, working hard in good faith, can make a mistake and be subject to fines, indictments, or other legal repercussions. It is a splendid example of how "ignorance of the law is no excuse." Even if your lawyer vets what you're doing and declares it legitimate, it's still you soliciting payment, so it's you who will face the music.

That being said, lawmakers understand the consequences of Draconian measures in a free marketplace, and so they have established exceptions to the rules. These exceptions have enabled physicians to expand their practices, consolidate spaces, share expenses, and be more efficient from a business standpoint.

Exceptions to the Stark Law

When a physician is looking to make a referral, it's straightforward as to where he must tread carefully. But what about a physician in a group practice?

According to the Stark statutes, the group practice can qualify for several exceptions, such as referrals to ancillary services in-office. But it must meet all of the Stark statutes' conditions as per its definition of a group practice:

1. The practice must have at least two or more physicians in a partnership, professional corporation, foundation, nonprofit corporation, or other comparable association.

2. Each physician, shareholder, partner, and employee group member (except independent contractors) must provide substantially (at least 75 percent) their normal full range of DHS via shared office space, facilities, equipment, and personnel.

   Careful! Considering this "full range," there is a "full range of service" test that everyone must meet. For example, if a group hires a part-time dermatologist only to treat alopecia but does the full range of dermatology in his own office, then his participation in the group would not be "full range." Therefore, the group wouldn't qualify as a group, and all the referrals for hair loss would violate Stark.

3. The practice must function as a unified business. This means a central decision-making group within the practice must control assets, budgets, salaries, etc.

4. There must be consolidated billing.

5. There must be a centralized utilization review.

6. Physicians may share in the group's profits and even be allowed a productivity bonus, as long as it isn't related to the volume or value of DHS referred by those physicians. In other words, no one can be rewarded for just the referrals.

7. All services by the group must be billed by "the group," e.g., a single group billing number and a single taxpayer identification number.

8. There must be rules in the distribution of overhead liability and income. These can't be changed in arrears when convenient but can only be adjusted going forward.

A referral for further edification is defined as any request from a physician or from within a physician group for (1) a service or article that is payable under Part B of Medicare, (2) a referral for a consultation and even all of the services ordered as a result of that consultation, and (3) a prescription for a course of treatment using DHS.

Further Exceptions to the Stark Laws

Every dark cloud has a silver lining.
—Poet, John Milton, *Comus*, 1634

- **The "Whole Hospital" Exception**: This allows physicians to make referrals to entities that are part of a whole hospital as long as the hospital is publicly traded or government owned.

- **The "Rural Provider" Exception**: This allows physicians in rural areas to make referrals to entities in which they have a financial interest, as long as the entities are located in the same rural area as the physician's practice. This makes it possible to practice in what are seen as areas of need or areas with underserved populations.

- **The "Group Practice" Exception (see above):** This exception allows physicians who are part of a group practice to make referrals to entities in which they have a financial interest as long as the group practice meets the requirements.

It is important to note that the physician and their practice are responsible for ensuring compliance with these laws.

"Don't do the crime if you can't do the time." Violations of the Stark law can result in serious penalties, including fines, exclusion from federal healthcare programs for decades, and even criminal charges when other statutes, e.g., the Anti-Kickback Statutes, are violated. Also, the law allows for whistleblowing by allowing private individuals and organizations to file lawsuits against physicians and entities that violate the laws, resulting in significant financial damages.

The government has beefed up enforcement of the Stark laws, now including participation by the Office of Inspector General (OIG) and the Department of Justice (DOJ), leading to active investigations and prosecution of violators. The OIG and DOJ have also increased the use of False Claims Act (FCA) lawsuits, which allow the government to recover penalties and damages from violators of the Stark law.

In summary, the Stark law is a federal law that prohibits physicians from making referrals for certain designated health services to entities in which they or their immediate family have a financial interest.

The good ol' days of letting your business seek profit any way it wanted are long over. The Stark mindset means well in the balance of over-bureaucratization vs. laissez-faire business ethics. But you have to remember that while under scrutiny, you're playing with the big boys now, and they can hammer you.

To a man with a hammer, everything looks like a nail.
—American psychologist Abraham Maslow

To avoid potential violations of the Stark law, become familiar with the laws and requirements. Consult with legal counsel when you need clarification about the law's applicability to your practice. Know the potential risks associated with making referrals to companies in which you have a financial interest.

The following chapters will discuss the ugly twin of the Stark laws: the dreaded anti-kickback laws. Stark exceptions establish what is considered permissible, i.e., remedying a prohibition only by complying with an exception. On the other hand, the anti-kickback safe harbor regulations are about transactions that may lead to referrals but don't necessarily violate the law. The safe harbor regulations even admit that transactions not meeting a safe harbor don't necessarily violate them—that's for a prosecutor to determine, which is pretty scary when you think about it.

CHAPTER 9

ANTI-KICKBACK STATUTE (AKS)

To be content with little is difficult; to be content with much, impossible.
—Marie von Ebner-Eschenbach

In Chapter 8, I discussed Stark laws, which have evolved and gelled from different contributions on various levels of ongoing legislation. The Stark laws are never quite finished, because our world is changing or because there are kinks and loopholes that keep cropping up, thanks to unscrupulous persons. Currently, they're in what is referred to as "Phase 3."

One of those kinks, to which I alluded last chapter, was the issue of kickbacks, whether they're a direct deposit in recognition (i.e., gratitude), a reward or unwritten contractual arrangement of payments, or even gifts of any type for referrals for services within the federal healthcare system. Impossible-to-get Broadway tickets are included in the broad spectrum of such items.

And thus, the Anti-Kickback Statute was engendered from the clumsy homunculus that was the original Social Security Act.

The Timeline

A powerful process automatically takes care of progress, productivity, and profits.
—Indian author Amit Kalantri, from *Wealth of Words*

1972: The federal Anti-Kickback Statute (AKS) was, as it turned out, an afterthought. Congress established the AKS in 1972 to address things not covered in original federal program legislation. As such, it is noteworthy that the original provisions were amendments to the Social Security Act. It, like Stark, has been amended many times.

1987: The Medicare and Medicaid Patient and Program Protection Act of 1987 specified various "safe harbors," i.e., payment practices, which, although possibly inducing referrals within Medicare or a state healthcare program, would be protected from criminal prosecution or civil sanctions.

1989: When the Stark law began as the Ethics in Patient Referrals Act, it failed even to garner a vote. However, it was vivisected, and portions were allotted to several Omnibus Budget Reconciliation Acts in 1989 and 1993 (i.e., Stark I and Stark II; currently, we're at Stark III).

The AKS is extremely broad. The types of remuneration prohibited include bribes and kickbacks made either directly or indirectly, in the open or in secret, in cash or in kind, on this planet or any other. In addition, it prohibited not only remuneration for referrals of patients but remuneration that also induced purchasing, leasing, ordering, or arranging for any goods, services, facilities, or items paid for by Medicare or state-funded health care programs. Thus, the AKS applies to any individual or entity that participates in or conducts business with these programs, including physicians, hospitals, nursing homes, and even pharmaceutical companies.

Since the statute was so broad, concern arose among many healthcare providers (all of them!) that many innocent commercial arrangements were subject to criminal prosecution. See "The Rest of the AKS Story" below.

The Difference Between Stark and the Anti-Kickback Statute

What's the difference? Both the Stark law and the Anti-Kickback Statute (AKS) are within the universe of federal healthcare programs, e.g., Medicare and Medicaid. However:

1. the Stark law applies only to referrals from physicians for services (i.e., designated health services) benefitting people connected to the referring physicians (immediate and extended family) and who would thereby profit from those referrals; but

2. the AKS applies to any referral regarding *any expenditure* that any federal government healthcare program will pay for.

While Stark is a civil offense, violating the AKS is a felony, which can send you to jail. A conviction might mean up to $25,000 in fines per violation—and incarceration for up to a five-year prison term. Or both!

It can even get worse. Read on.

What's Verboten?

Verboten is defined as you cannot (knowingly or willfully) offer, pay, solicit, or receive anything of value to encourage or reward referrals to federal healthcare programs. While a restaurateur, for instance, can offer a patron a complimentary appetizer for bringing their ten friends to the restaurant for the annual Christmas dinner, that would be a serious crime in the healthcare industry.

In many industries, it's kosher—even clever marketing—to reward people who send you business. However, many with a distrustful mindset felt it could influence how care was rendered by an otherwise noble profession. Lawmakers were concerned that kickbacks and bribes to physicians could pervert medical decision-making. It can, and it has.

The Rest of the AKS Story

The AKS was extremely broad. It specifically outlawed kickbacks, bribes, and rebates made directly or indirectly, overtly or covertly (i.e., with a wink or not), in cash, or other ways, *viz*, the Broadway tickets. Besides rewarding such things for referrals, it also outlawed payoffs made to seduce the purchasing, leasing, ordering, or arranging for any goods, facilities, services, or items paid for by federal or state healthcare programs. "Any goods, etc." is the main difference (and refinement) of the Stark law.

Since the statute was so broad, many healthcare providers feared criminal prosecution by overzealous prosecutors for even innocent commercial arrangements. So in 1987, the Medicare and Medicaid Patient and Program Protection Act was revised with two new provisions:

It allowed the Office of the Inspector General (OIG) new authority to kick a provider out of all federal and state programs as an alternative to adjudicating a felony; that is, an alternative civil remedy short of criminal prosecution;

Secondly, it specified payment practices that wouldn't be subject to criminal prosecution. Translation: the government tried to make health care practice not so damned scary.

Softening of the felonious rhetoric included specifying how to structure some "payoffs" as safe harbors, such as hospitals granting office space that could be interpreted as a kickback for referrals.

Still, despite reducing the burden of fear, AKS has gnarly teeth: If a medical device manufacturer wants to reward a physician for using that device during surgeries, they could provide lavish vacations, pay sizeable "consulting fees," or pay for panel involvement in its speaker bureau. In this case, the government could prosecute both the company and the physician. Instead of Club Med, we would be talking about Club Fed.

In addition, the law allows private citizens and organizations to sue you, too, which can result in significant financial damages. This comes awfully close to a whistleblower's mandate.

'Cause the night has a thousand eyes
And a thousand eyes can't help but see if you are true to me
So remember when you tell those little white lies
That the night has a thousand eyes.
–Bobby Vee, "The Night Has a Thousand Eyes"

Safe Harbors

Yet even the established safe harbors were judged to be excessively narrow—or should I say, shallow? Therefore, in 1989 they were widened (or dredged deeper) in ten broad areas that had arisen on the felonious radar:

1. **Investment Interests**: A safe harbor provision was proposed for investment interests in large public corporations where such investments are available to the general public.

2. **Rent**: A safe harbor provision was proposed for rental arrangements, according to rent intervals of at least a year, based on fair market value and not the number of referred patients.

3. **Equipment Rental**: To avoid using diagnostic and other equipment as reimbursement for referrals, fair market value and other conditions, as applied to rent above, were implemented.

4. **Personal Services and Management Contracts**: This established a safe harbor for joint ventures and other arrangements involving payments for personal services or management contracts, but only with specific standards that discourage financial incentives for referrals. It allows certain types of contracts between healthcare providers, such as contracts for managing or operating a facility or providing personal services. Again, fair market value was essential to any such arrangement.

5. **Sale of Practice**: This was to discourage a "retiring" physician from selling to a hospital but then continuing to practice within it as a source of ongoing referrals to that hospital.

6. **Referral Services**: This established a safe harbor for professional societies and other consumer groups to operate referral services for a fee, but only when several standards were met.

7. **Warranties**: A safe harbor was allowed when warranties are offered as an inducement for customers when it is in the public interest.

8. **Discounts**: While not sanctioning cash rebates, free services, or credit, a safe harbor was defined as relating to discounts for employees and group purchasing organizations in recognition of the benefits to Medicare and Medicaid that competition confers.

9. **Employees**: This established an exception for rewarding employees for assisting in solicitation.

10. **Group Purchasing Organizations (GPOs):** This enabled payments from vendors to GPOs for providers providing Medicare or Medicaid services, as long as the agreement is in writing and specifies the details of amounts.

Also, there is a "rural provider" exception, which allows for certain types of financial arrangements between healthcare providers in rural areas as long as the arrangements meet certain requirements. This is designed to encourage practice in underserved areas.

Everything here should be followed by a very insistent disclaimer:

These are very simplified; a suitably qualified healthcare lawyer can only appreciate the full extent of each.

You are protected from liability when you structure an arrangement to "dock" in a safe harbor. While compliance with safe harbors is voluntary, doing so assures safety from those watching you carefully.

Bear in mind that all of these exceptions and safe harbors have exact requirements that must be met for the individual or entity to comply with the AKS. The individual or entity is responsible for ensuring compliance with these laws. If you're wheelin' and dealin', you need to know the rules.

Is Healthcare Really Us vs. Them?

The purpose of the AKS is to ensure that healthcare decisions are in the patients' best interests only. AKS considers financial incentives mortal sins. It is designed to ensure what's best for the patient and what's best for the taxpayers who fund the federal and state healthcare programs.

But make no mistake. Regulatory agencies love their jobs. They love to catch "bad guys." Where the line between dutiful and overzealous is drawn favors the person drawing that line.

Rule of law is the grey area between the two extremes, *viz* the moral norm of individual liberty and state coercion. When it is at the former end, it is anarchy; when at the latter, it is a totalitarian repressive state. In the real world, every state operates somewhere between these two extremes.
—Author R. N. Prasher

If you get into the crosshairs, your career (or freedom) will never be the same. Even if all you get is the slap on the wrist of being barred from Medicare or Medicaid for fifteen years (and that is some slap), you'll never treat anyone over sixty-five again since life expectancy is ever-rising, that will be more and more the patient base of your practice. And that's just Medicare. Want to admit a patient to a hospital that accepts Medicaid? Even if your care is under other arrangements, forget it. The exclusion authority provided for by AKS can literally put you out of business.

How Bad Can It Get?

The False Claims Act

Kickback violations can lead to indictments based on the False Claims Act. This civil statute allows the government to recover money it feels you received illegally, with a catch: you can be assessed up to three times the federal program's loss, plus $11,000 per claim. As you can see, such penalties can add up quickly.

The Civil Monetary Penalties Law

This allows the OIG to subject you to a civil monetary penalty of $50,000 per violation and up to three times the total amount of the kickback payments, even if some parts were legitimate.

> The architects of this wickedness will find no safe harbor in this world. We will chase our enemies to the furthest corners of this Earth. It must be war without quarter, pursuit without rest, victory without qualification.
> —Former US Representative, former House Majority Leader, and former felon Tom DeLay

---

If you're a "wicked architect" in how you engage in health care, know that the government has increased its enforcement of AKS, with the OIG and DOJ actively investigating and prosecuting violators. The OIG and DOJ have also increased the use of lawsuits under the False Claims Act, allowing them to go after what helps fund them: money from damages and penalties.

It would be best if you familiarized yourself with these laws and statutes, their requirements, what they allow, and what they don't allow. But unless you're a healthcare lawyer, you should always consult with specialized legal counsel when unsure about the law's applicability to your practice or business. If you're a restaurateur, fine. But if not, you should always weigh the potential risks associated with accepting or providing anything of value in exchange for referrals—or the appearance of taking anything in exchange for referrals.

You're not a bad person, but nothing is as personally unsettling as reviewing your behavior after you're targeted and realizing you just might have done something that was bad—accidentally or accidentally on purpose.

Even if you have all your charges dismissed, as Tom DeLay finally did, your life will never be the same.

But wait. It just got uglier.

A bastard child of the AKS is a spine-chilling entity called the Travel Act. Briefly, suppose kickback laws are violated by providers involved in an entity that does not take federally funded patients. In that case, the DOJ can still come after you and prosecute you if the violations are egregious enough in nature. They do so by invoking the Travel Act.

The Travel Act was enacted in the early 1960s to prevent racketeering activities stemming from organized crime. It forbids knowingly using any facility in interstate or foreign dealing with the intent to distribute the proceeds of an unlawful activity or facilitate an unlawful activity. In simple terms, the act puts the illegality of committing criminal acts across state lines in place, acts that can take place via email or other electronic methods. The Travel Act has not traditionally been used in the healthcare context. Still, it does give the government the power to federalize state crimes and consider whether private, commercial insurance arrangements comply with federal criminal law. Patient referral cases involving private insurance have traditionally escaped this prosecutorial scrutiny since most federal enforcement actions focused on federal healthcare programs. Insurance Fraud & Federal Prosecutions – Fort Lauderdale Criminal Defense Attorney. https://www.thelawdesk.com/insurance-fraud-federal-prosecutions/ Well, not anymore.

A federal jury found seven defendants in *United States v. Beauchamp*, connected with the Forest Park Medical Center (FPMC) in Dallas, Texas, guilty of conspiring to pay or receive health care kickbacks in April 2019. The defendants were convicted of collecting over $200 million in a kickback scheme where doctors were paid to refer patients to FPMC. Both the AKS and the Travel Act were invoked to pursue these cases. The interesting thing in this case is that no federally funded patients or services were involved in this scheme by the perpetrators. How did the DOJ prosecute them? The government alleged that coconspirators used email instructions and a Federal Reserve Bank's computer network to send bribes and kickback payments...holy s***! Is nothing unsacred anymore?

The broader use of the Travel Act has sent shivers down all the collective spines of healthcare attorneys because that vastly broadens the brush-stroke the federal government can use to prosecute healthcare providers. Basically, every act you do is under scrutiny and on the table for the government. The rules just got rewritten.

Conclusion

While the tone of this chapter seems anti-this and anti-that, we must trust that laws are made in good faith. If you think living with laws is challenging, try living without them.

> It's all very well to run around saying regulation is bad, get the government off our backs, etc. Of course, our lives are regulated. When you come to a stop sign, you stop; if you want to go fishing, you get a license; if you want to shoot ducks, you can shoot only three ducks. The alternative is dead bodies at the intersection, no fish, and no ducks.
> —American newspaper columnist Mary Tyler "Molly" Ivins

The federal Anti-Kickback Statute prohibits exchanging anything valuable, directly or indirectly, in an effort to prompt or remunerate referrals for items or services covered in federal healthcare programs such as Medicare and Medicaid. The law was intended to prevent fraud and abuse in the healthcare system, and, in all fairness, it has tried to remedy some of the unfair fallout from such vigilance with the continuing refinement of its safe harbors. On the clinical side of things, these laws and statutes ensure that healthcare decisions are made in the patient's best interests—and there's nothing wrong with that. You took an oath, remember? And while that Hippocratic Oath is largely symbolic, the law is not!

CHAPTER 10

ANTITRUST LAWS

First they came for the Communists
And I did not speak out
Because I was not a Communist
Then they came for the Socialists
And I did not speak out
Because I was not a Socialist
Then they came for the trade unionists
And I did not speak out
Because I was not a trade unionist
Then they came for the Jews
And I did not speak out
Because I was not a Jew
Then they came for me
And there was no one left
To speak out for me
– Pastor Martin Niemöller

In the United States, antitrust law is a collection of largely federal laws that govern company activity and organization to foster competition and avoid unjustified monopolies. Antitrust laws are the broad group of state and federal laws designed to ensure businesses compete fairly. The *trust* in antitrust refers to a group of businesses that team up or form a monopoly to dictate pricing in a particular market.

The federal antitrust laws that most often affect medical providers are the Sherman Act and Section 7 of the Clayton Act. The Sherman Act comprises two sections; Section 1 deals with conspiracies to restrain trade and applies to price fixing and group boycotts, and Section 2 deals with illegal monopolies. Under Section 2 of the Sherman Act, an illegal monopoly is willfully acquired by predatory conduct or other unlawful means. Section 7 of the Clayton Act prohibits the merger of two or more entities that may result in reduced competition and may be implicated when physician practices merge, and the combination is large enough, relative to the specific community, to lead to less competition in the market.

While superficially, it seems that these complicated laws and rules only apply to industry behemoths, the sad fact of life is that most healthcare businesses and entities we are part of are subject to antitrust laws and their perceived violation, if any. It behooves an investor well to know these laws, know how to avoid committing their violation, and avoid any situation that may subject them to scrutiny under these laws.

Introduction: Who Do You Trust?

> Which shall rule—wealth or man? Which shall lead—money or intellect? Who shall fill public stations—educated and patriotic freemen or the feudal serfs of corporate capital?
> —Edward G. Ryan, 19th Century Chief Justice of Wisconsin

Do you trust labor unions? Insurance companies? How about baseball?

The US government does, because these three things are exempt from its antitrust laws. Everything else, that's a matter of debate—sometimes even in the Supreme Court. Just ask Google. Better yet, Google it.

Antitrust isn't a matter of trust or even distrusting trust. Trust is a concept of reliance and confidence. It is an ideal. But to 1882 oil refiner John D. Rockefeller, a trust—his, called the Standard Oil Trust—was a centralizing legal loophole to acquire industries across state lines. Thus, Rockefeller is the guy who made monopoly a dirty word.

He and the tycoons of the "good ol' days" hijacked the nation's entire economy. The result was wage cuts, violence in job actions, and economic collapse. Like all good ol' days, those days ended. (Are you listening, Ticketmaster?)

How to Clean a Dirty Word

In 1887, the railroad-riding public had had it. They wanted fair fees and transparent standardization of them. The Interstate Commerce Act gave them that.

However, in 1890, US Senator John Sherman of Ohio introduced the Sherman Act to outlaw contracts that restrained trade, agreed upon behind closed doors in conspiracies to monopolize industries, fix prices, divide and conquer markets, and rig bidding. Sherman wanted to refine the vigilance and began with the Interstate Commerce Act.

Twenty-four years later, the 1914 Federal Trade Commission Act banned unjust competition and deceptive methods. Also that year, the Clayton Act was passed, closing more loopholes the Sherman Act suffered. For example, Clayton forbade choosing the same person to make decisions for competing corporations.

Cleaning a Dirty Word—Throwing the Baby Out with the Bathwater

Under the antitrust laws, a man becomes a criminal from the moment he goes into business...if he charges prices which some bureaucrats judge as too high, he can be prosecuted for..."intent to monopolize," if he charges prices lower than those of his competitors, he can be prosecuted for "unfair competition" or "restraint of trade," and if he charges the same prices as his competitors, he can be prosecuted for "collusion" or "conspiracy."

—Ayn Rand, objectivist author

While Ayn Rand's anti-statist objectivism caused her to think of government benefits as an immoral redistribution, she nonetheless received social security in her later years. If you think people are complicated, it's nothing compared to commerce. With Rand's family having been ruined by the Bolsheviks in her native Russia, she vehemently opposed all federal regulations that suggested you be generous, but at gunpoint.

It is only a slight exaggeration to say that the average busy professional in this country wakes up in the morning, goes to work, comes home, takes care of personal and family obligations, and then goes to sleep, unaware that he or she likely committed several federal crimes that day.

—Author Harvey Silverglate, *Three Felonies a Day: How the Feds Target the Innocent*

Big-Ticket Items

Transportation, manufacturing, marketing, and distribution are all big-ticket items that are fraught with abuse, which unfortunately trickles down to the paying customer, client, or—in the case of healthcare—the patients or the provider who cares for them.

Healthcare keeps reinventing itself, as any healthy capitalistic enterprise will. For every government action, there is an opposite but not always equal business reaction. As such, healthcare as an industry kept getting bigger and bigger. As it did, the FTC and DOJ reared their officious heads to protect consumers from the anticompetitive practices of healthcare companies.

> We the People of the United States, in Order to form a more perfect Union, establish Justice, insure domestic Tranquility, provide for the common defense, promote the general Welfare, and secure the Blessings of Liberty to ourselves and our Posterity, do ordain and establish this Constitution for the United States of America.
> –"Preamble," United States Constitution

Today, now that the major kinks of railroading, telephone dialing, and pumping gas have been straightened somewhat, healthcare is the new big-ticket item du jour. The FTC is particularly wary of mergers and acquisitions and wants to be looking into the microscope before things even start.

To ensure any proposed merger or intended acquisition doesn't create a combined Goliath with too much market power, the ability to raise or fix prices, or reduce the quality of its products or services, the FTC and DOJ review any proposed mergers or acquisitions. Officious, yes, but in the constitutional sense of "promoting the general welfare," it is the vehicle by which competition is protected, as are those who should benefit from a brisk competitive market.

The vilest example of extreme merging or acquisition is that which results in a monopoly. In 1974, AT&T monopolized the telephone market. By the time it was broken up into AT&T Inc., Verizon, and Qwest, a funny thing happened to telephones. They got better. (Constitutionally, "more perfect.")

Under AT&T's monopoly, phone dials remained unchanged for almost fifty years. Suddenly, there appeared pushbuttons, keypads, touchtone, call-waiting, and all of the seminal pushes toward the magic we have today, called cellular devices. Magic devices.

Any sufficiently advanced technology is
indistinguishable from magic.
–Author and futurist Arthur C. Clarke

The world indeed changed, and without antitrust, we'd probably still be dialing on party lines. (What are party lines?) We'd still be paying a whole lot for toll calls. It used to be that dialing out of your area code—even the one next door—was deemed long distance. This all plays into an epiphany of sorts: competition not only lowers prices but also improves commodities. And it can even do both simultaneously.

The number of transistors on a microchip doubles about
every two years, though the cost of computers is halved.
–"Moore's Law," 1965, attributed to Gordon Moore,
cofounder of Intel

Price Fixing and Exclusivity

When purchasers make choices about what products and services to buy, they expect that the price has been determined on the basis of supply and demand, not by an agreement among competitors.
—Federal Trade Commission, on price fixing

According to the FTC, when it comes to prices we pay, the market should decide, not those who intend to manipulate it. As such, another concern is price fixing, where healthcare providers or companies agree to charge the same prices for their products or services. This can lead to prices never going down at best and higher prices for consumers at worst, making competition obsolete.

The FTC and DOJ also investigate and prosecute price-fixing cases in the healthcare industry. The scrutiny has become so intense that most companies/corporations enlist counsel from legal experts before jumping into anything. (And so should you. Good advice, always.)

One example of anticompetitive behavior is exclusive dealing, in which a company requires a customer or supplier to do business with only them instead of allowing for shopping around for the best prices or services. Alternatively, it is also exclusive dealing when one business puts conditions on another's complete freedom to choose what it buys or sells. For example, if an ambulatory surgery center is given the opportunity to buy heavily discounted disposable items if—and only if—it refuses to use a competitor's disposable items for sale.

Another example of exclusive dealing is the concept of *tying*. This is a type of bundling in which a seller makes buying something conditioned by buying something else in a package deal. For example, a requirements tie-in sale occurs when the seller requires customers who purchase one product from the seller (e.g., a printer) also to make all their purchases of other items (e.g., ink cartridges) part of the deal. This could encourage sellers to base what they charge on how much products are used.

Price-fixing, exclusive dealing, bundling, tying, etc., create an insider game that others cannot play. You only get to decide whether you're an insider or not if you're part of the problem, of course. Economics mandates that these nefarious machinations limit competition and drive prices up for unfairly ostracized consumers.

Beware: The Even Playing Field Tilts

In the healthcare industry, there are concerns over the negotiation of prices between healthcare providers and the health insurance companies that reimburse them for their services. Insurance companies often have more negotiating power than individual providers, which can lead to lower reimbursement rates and reduced access to care.

The FTC monitors the healthcare payer industry to ensure these negotiations do not harm competition. However, you must realize that the insurance industry is one of those which, in the past, have been exempt from antitrust laws. This is because the federal government had considered the states' regulations good enough. To challenge this overoptimistic stance, you need go no further than the state of Louisiana, where three of its four previous insurance commissioners were convicted and incarcerated due to crimes within their office. (Louisiana: flood insurance, anyone?)

Before President Trump signed CHIRA (the Competitive Health Insurance Reform Act), both Aetna and Blue Cross/Blue Shield—as theoretical examples—could agree not to put a particular provider on either of their provider panels, which (if it were you) could severely impact your ability to make a living. Yet, you and another doctor are not allowed to agree to refuse to treat patients of any one particular insurance company. After all, that's a conspiracy. Why?

Because insurance is gambling, and what happens in Vegas...well...

The 1945 McCarran-Ferguson Act exempted certain insurer activities from antitrust criticism when they were doing what is considered "the business of insurance." Therefore, insurance business is not equivalent to boycott, coercion, or intimidation. As such, the business of insurance is conduct that spreads a policyholder's risk, is integral to the policy between the insured and insurer, and can only be done within the insurance industry.

This exemption gave the blessing to cooperative rate-making efforts (aka, conspiracy), development of standard policy forms (aka, linking and bundling), joint underwriting (aka, price fixing), decisions to accept or deny insurance applications (aka, discrimination and profiling), claims handling (aka, price fixing), and reinsurance (aka, exclusion). The house always wins.

Yet, you and another provider still cannot conspire against any insurer. Those who opposed CHIRA included the National Association of Insurance Commissioners, and we know where some of them are.

Who Else is Exempt? Who's On First?

Who else is exempt?

Unions won the right to strike in 1914's Clayton Act and were granted the right to band together.

> The labor of a human being is not a commodity or article of commerce. Nothing contained in the antitrust laws shall be construed to forbid the existence and operation of labor... organizations...nor shall such organizations, or the members thereof, be held or construed to be illegal combinations or conspiracies in restraint of trade under the antitrust laws.
> —Section 6 of the Clayton Act

Unions and politics have been bedfellows forever, regardless of which side of the bed you woke up on.

Baseball is exempt because, well...it's just a game and not commerce. Right? So said the Supreme Court back in 1923, when Babe Ruth was hitting homers. Some things are just plain sacred.

> Baseball was, is, and always will be to me
> the best game in the world.
> —B. Ruth, Yankee, Brave, and red-sock-wearer

David and Goliath

Hospitals still abuse small medical businesses. Large hospital systems' actions negatively impact the financial health and growth potential of providers' medical practices and industries. This can include a variety of indiscretions, such as:

1. **Anticompetitive Behavior**: Large hospitals or hospital systems engage in exclusive contracts with insurance companies or suppliers, making it difficult for smaller medical businesses to compete.

Yet, if you are on the staff of said hospital, an insurance company can still keep you away from their patients, even though they go to the same hospital who has credentialed you.

2. **Price Fixing**: Large hospital systems may scheme with other providers to fix service prices. Only when someone blows the whistle on such an activity can it be easier for smaller medical businesses to charge competitive prices. That being said, the government itself has made it harder to blow that whistle.

   With Medicare's setting of its own reasonable and customary rates (UCRs), private insurers have hidden behind these pricing structures as the "law of the land," even when their previous reimbursements exceeded Medicare's.

3. **Forced Buyouts**: Large hospital systems may use their financial resources to force smaller medical businesses to sell to them, which can limit competition and lead to higher prices for patients. But this may not be the only motive; it also can drive providers who refuse to sell out of the market altogether, which is the ultimate endpoint of limiting competition.

4. **Physician Steering**: Large hospital systems may steer patients away from smaller medical enterprises, limiting their patient bases and making it difficult for them to grow.

   The emergency department is a good example of a steer-worthy department of a large hospital. Follow-up care can be referred to preferred providers.

5. **Unfair Reimbursement Rates**: Large hospital systems may negotiate higher reimbursement rates with insurance companies, making it difficult for small medical businesses to be reimbursed fairly.

It may seem like apples and oranges to these two players, but it's all green to you. These practices can make it difficult for small medical businesses to survive, and with fewer players in the game (with apologies to Babe Ruth), this can lead to loftier healthcare costs for patients. Government regulators need to monitor and take action to prevent hospital abuse of small medical businesses to ensure a competitive marketplace and fair healthcare prices for patients.

On the other hand, how can a doctor or entry-level healthcare investor violate these laws without even having the nefarious acumen of the big players? Here are some examples:

1. **Price Fixing**: When doctors and their practices collude with other groups to set prices for their services at a certain level, it can harm competition and lead to higher patient costs.

2. **Market Allocation**: When doctors and their groups agree to divide up markets or patients, it can limit competition and reduce patient choices.

3. **Group Boycotts**: When doctors team up and agree to refuse to deal with certain competitors or insurance plans, it can limit competition and reduce patient choices. This is possibly the saddest application of the antitrust laws.

4. **Refusals to Deal**: When a group of doctors refuses to work with certain hospitals or healthcare providers, it can limit competition and reduce patient options. Again, someone centuries back meant well, but the laws in most of these instances nowadays are used to stifle options for clinicians.

5. **Tying Arrangements**: When a doctor requires patients to use certain products or services in conjunction with their medi-

cal services, it can limit competition and force patients to buy products they may not need or want.

Conclusion

Overall, antitrust laws in healthcare aim to ensure fair competition and protect consumers from anticompetitive practices. The FTC and DOJ actively enforce these laws and investigate potential violations to prevent monopolies and promote competition in the healthcare industry. They have successfully taken on the Rockefellers, Alcoa Aluminum, the railroads, telephone companies, and Google. Don't get on their bad side because you will be very insignificant in comparison. But the one good thing is that they're after everybody, including your enemies: insurers and large hospitals. And an enemy of your enemy is your friend.

Fate gives all of us three teachers, three friends, three enemies, and three great loves in our lives. But these twelve are always disguised, and we can never know which one is which until we've loved them, left them, or fought them.
—Novelist Gregory David Roberts, *Shantaram*

To the average healthcare entrepreneur out there: anytime you raise your voice to right an ill, anytime you congregate with other businesspeople to form an alliance, and anytime you grab an opportunity to improve on your profits, beware the Medusa heads of the antitrust laws focusing their serpentine stares at you.

CHAPTER 11

FINANCIAL PRINCIPLES OF ACQUISITION

The noblest pleasure is the joy of understanding.
—Leonardo da Vinci

Much like the universe in general, the business world runs on mathematical formulas. A great thing about arithmetic is that it works. It's consistent, and it's reliable. It is why it is used in formulas at all. The above are formulas used to value a business, and where they fit will make sense in the "Basic Principles of Valuating a Business" section below.

Determining the value of a business is, of course, the most important aspect of whether you proceed or let an opportunity pass. Thus, valuing the business is critical in buying or selling a company. It is calculated using a combination of its financial performance and assets, along with intangibles such as the current market conditions and emerging trends in the industry.

The formulas I mention aren't necessarily the chronological or all-inclusive steps in valuing a business but are part of the overall language within the process. Your buyer (or seller) will be throwing them around, so it's best to have a working knowledge of them.

What Are the Steps in Determining the Value of a Business?

There are key steps involved in valuing a business for possible purchase. The same steps will be used "at" you for selling your business. Whichever direction the flow goes—buying or selling—the steps are the same, just with a different vector, respectively.

Data beats emotions.
—Sean Rad, founder of Tinder

Previously, EBITDA was introduced:

EBITDA = Revenue (total income generated by the business)

– Cost of Goods Sold	(direct costs associated with producing the goods)
– Operating Expenses	(indirect cost of running the business)
+ Depreciation	(decrease in value of assets over time)
+ Amortization	(gradual write-off of intangible assets)

EBITDA remains the gold standard for a quick business assessment, valuation, and analysis. However, we use other parameters to assess a business's value. Another commonly used formula is Net Present Value (NPV), used in conjunction with the EBITDA:

Net Present Value (NPV) = (PV of Future Cash Flows) – (Initial Investment) where PV of Future Cash Flows is the present value of expected future cash flows and Initial Investment is the initial cost of purchasing the business.

In addition to the above, your actuary and accountants will depend on other formulas and tools to truly evaluate the worth of your future venture. A few worth mentioning are:

1. The P/E Ratio formula:

   (Market Price per Share ÷ Earning per Share)

   - Market Price per Share = the present stock price of the business
   - Earnings per Share = (Net Income of the Business) ÷ (Number of Outstanding Shares)

2. The Discounted Cash Flow (DCF) formula:

   $(CF1) \div (1 + r)^1 + (CF2) \div (1 + r)^2 \ldots + (CFn) \div (1 + r)^n$

   - CF = the cash flow expected in each year of investment
   - r = the discount rate (i.e., the required rate of return)
   - n = the number of years of the investment

3. Return on Investment (ROI) formula:

   (Gain from Investment – Cost of Investment) ÷ (Cost of Investment ′ 100%)

   - Gain from Investment = the income received from the investment
   - Cost of Investment = the total cost of the investment

While these formulas help the actuaries assess your future investment, you don't have to be a mathematical genius to do your own due diligence in purchasing a business. For an investor, here are some key steps for valuing a business:

1. **Evaluate Financial Statements**: The first step in valuing a business is to examine its financial statements, including the balance sheet and the income and cash flow statements. This will help you understand the company's revenue, expenses, and profitability.

Examining previous financial statements, perhaps a few iterations back, is also useful. This will give you practical insight into how the current owner self-scores the business's worth over time. It also can display some red flags if you see unnatural or impossible jumps in the arithmetic over some set time. (This primarily applies to buying a business. Unless you're asked, it's neither prudent nor necessary to volunteer these if you're the one who's selling.)

I was recently asked to opine on the purchase value of an aviation company in the Midwest. The seller showed a modest profit in recent years and artfully blamed the losses mentioned in his three-year summary on COVID-19. It took a step further for us to probe and discover that poor COVID-19 (yes, that sounds like an oxymoron) had nothing to do with his years of lackluster performance.

2. **Assess the Company's Assets**: The value of a business is also determined by its assets, such as property, equipment, and inventory. It's essential to accurately assess these assets' values to determine the business's overall value.

   Inventory turnover is a dynamic process, so the numbers you see represent only a snapshot. You will need to gestalt this snapshot along with the industry trends and market conditions. Don't assume any number is fixed; some numbers will be more versatile or volatile than others.

   For example, property value is a slowly changing metric, yet the equipment value—slow, too—changes a bit faster than property. Property value also depends on trends since the maxim "location, location, location" will change in relevance as an urban or suburban landscape, zoning, politics, or demographics change.

Another asset is the online presence and how dynamic services can be dispersed into the ether. Web traffic is equity. Search engine optimization is valuable. If there is no significant Web presence, that can be a dangerous linchpin to pull on the value of a business. More than a linchpin, it might be like pulling the pin on a hand grenade!

Hey, watch this!
—famous last words

---

3. **Analyze Market Conditions**: Market conditions can significantly impact the value of a business. Factors that affect market conditions are:

    - **The Competition**: Are you considering buying a mom-and-pop shop next door to some big box mammoth? Again, comparing financial statements can tell you a lot about the competition, because winning or losing in the competition game will be reflected on financial statements over time.
    - **Supply and Demand**: There is so much that figures into this keystone concept of capitalism that it could fill an entirely new book. However, for our purposes here, it suffices to summarize some of the things that impact supply and demand.

As the recent COVID-19 pandemic so painfully illustrated, supply chains are the eight-hundred-pound gorillas in the room. Are these running smoothly? Have there been multiple changes in suppliers in a short amount of time (red flag)? Are there any international phenomena at work, e.g., trade sanctions involving countries upon which the supply depends? What about in the near future? (For example, there is nothing etched in cement over buying inventory from China, or Taiwan if it's invaded. Just a thought—paranoid, yes, but stranger things have happened. Hashtag "Ukraine.")

After the supply chain, you must consider any middlemen who grease it. Are there any problems with them? Next, there's demand, which isn't necessarily an eight-hundred-pound gorilla but is nonetheless a sizeable beast. Demand will fractionate, as if it weren't complicated enough, into what the supply chain delivers.

If the supply chain is optimal, this might work against you if there are a lot of products out there the same as yours. Supply is up, and demand is down. On the other hand, if it's compromised, you can capitalize on this if you can figure out a way to ensure you're at the top of that food chain. Be nice:

> If people like you, they'll listen to you, but if they trust you, they'll do business with you.
> —Zig Ziglar, author, salesman, and motivational speaker

You will do well if you have a lot of what others don't because of their own supply chain issues. Such a strategy, however, depends on your relationships with these providing suppliers, so be nice to them even during the fat times when you don't have to.

Also implicit in supply and demand is your turnover. Are the warehouses packed because the business can't get stuff to its customers fast enough? That is, is the company the problem? Everything is interconnected, and everything affects everything else.

Be undeniably good. No marketing effort or social media buzzword can be a substitute for that.
—Anthony Volodkin, founder of Hype Machine

Service remains key even if the business is a service provider instead of a commodity seller. Customers who have to wait will get what they want faster if available. In today's Internet of Things, it's just a keyword search away.

1. **Technology**: Changes in technology can affect the value of a company. An obvious direction to look at is the online presence mentioned in the "Assets" section above. But with total knowledge doubling faster than ever, technology is now part of every aspect of the business. There needs to be more than the proper hardware—the right software, which changes constantly, is also a must. These impact the entire business process, from the nitty gritty and wear-and-tear of durable equipment to the ghostlike machinations of online processing.

   But you must do more than go by Yelp or Amazon ratings. To have the best hardware and software for your business requires the help of consultants in the industry. It's impossible to keep up with where the tech is going otherwise. They charge, but pay for it. It's an education.

Education costs money. But then so does ignorance.
—Sir Claus Moser, statistician

It's a necessary investment, or you will wonder about the numbers on the financial statement that have evolved from unsuspected precursors, well hidden, farther up the enterprise tree.

2. **Consider the Industry**: The industry in which the business operates can also impact its value. For example, a business in a growing industry may be worth more than a business in a declining industry. Again, as I had previously snarked, think smartphones vs. rotary phones. Think terabytes instead of megabytes. Think gigahertz instead of the Pony Express.

The secret of change is to focus all your energy not on fighting the old but on building the new.
—Socrates, father of Western philosophy

See things in the present, even if they are in the future.
—Larry Ellison, cofounder of Oracle

Here's a genuinely terrifying trip down the recent memory lane of obsolescence: Using couriers instead of mail. Using faxes instead of couriers. Using email instead of faxes. And on and on…

Always look for the fool in the deal. If you don't find one, it's you.
—AXS TV chairman and entrepreneur Mark Cuban

Had you invested in a courier business or the fax manufacturing industry, you chose poorly.

Get a mentor in the applicable field if you're at all unsure of what you're looking for.
—Kyle Bragger, founder of Forrst and cofounder of Exposure

3. **Get Professional Help**: It's not just for picking software. Valuing a business can be a complex process, and it's vital to seek professional help from an accountant or business broker to ensure that the valuation is accurate and reliable.

Tangentially, there's the human factor. Is this a happy company? Can you tell even after the steps above indicate so? Look for toxic conditions.

Eating a toxic company will poison your future.
—Executive dyspeptic Ralph Ebe

We are what we eat.
—German philosopher Ludwig Feuerbach

The Basic Principles of Valuating a Business

Several different valuation methods can be used to value a business:

- Income approach
- Market approach
- Asset-based approach

Such are three common methods, each with advantages and disadvantages. The method most appropriate will depend on the specific circumstances of the business.

1. **Income Approach**: This method estimates the value of a business based on its ability to produce future income.

   The most common income approach is the Discounted Cash Flow (DCF) analysis, which estimates the current value of future cash flows the business is expected to generate.

   Discounted Cash Flow (DCF) formula is CF1 [÷] (1+r)^1 + CF2 [÷] (1 + r)^2 + ... + CFn [÷] (1 + r)^n

   - CF is the cash flow expected in each year of investment
   - "r" is the discount rate (i.e., the required rate of return)
   - "n" is the number of years of the investment

   This method involves forecasting the business's cash flows over time and then discounting them back to their current value using a discount rate that considers the time, value of money, and the risk of the investment.

2. **Market Approach**: This method estimates a company's value based on the market value of similar businesses.

   The most common market approach method is the comparable company analysis, which compares the financial standard of the business being appraised to those of similar recently sold or publicly traded companies. This method involves selecting a group of comparable companies, analyzing their financial metrics, and then applying those metrics to the business being valued to determine its value.

3. **Asset-Based Approach**: This method estimates a business's value based on the value of its assets. The most common asset approach method is the adjusted book value. It calculates the value of the business's assets based on their fair market value and subtracts any liabilities to arrive at its net asset value.

   This method is most appropriate for businesses with considerable tangible assets, such as real estate or equipment.

It's important to note that these methods are not mutually exclusive and can be combined to arrive at a more accurate valuation. Additionally, it's recommended to consult with a professional accountant or business broker to ensure the valuation is accurate and reliable. And lest you forget, make sure you have—or hire someone with—the latest software to compute these parameters.

Healthcare is an immortal beast. Until the end of time, healthcare will remain a viable business. For the most part, it is recession-proof, inflation-proof, pandemic-proof, and so on. As I will mention in later chapters on the specific entities a healthcare entrepreneur can invest in, you have a plethora of choices to pick from. You will not go wrong with what you choose. The strength or weakness of the specific business you take over can hurt your investment. Exercise due diligence. All that glitters is not gold, but gold always has at least some glitter. Find the glitter in the business. If there is none, it's not gold.

CHAPTER 12

THE DEBT ARCHITECTURE: USING OTHER PEOPLE'S MONEY TO BUILD MY EMPIRE

"Cash is a position, but leverage is a strategy."
– Ray Dalio

I was trained, like most physicians, to fear debt. In medical school and residency, debt meant vulnerability. It meant exposure. It meant risk. Somewhere along the way, I realized that this belief system was not accidental—it was inherited from a professional culture that rewards income but quietly punishes ownership. Debt, I learned, is not a moral failure. It is a tool. And in healthcare, it is the single most misunderstood tool of all.

When I finally stepped back and studied how large healthcare enterprises actually operate, the illusion shattered. Hospital systems do not avoid debt—they are built on it. The average nonprofit hospital system in the United States carries long-term debt equal to roughly 45–60% of total capitalization. Publicly traded healthcare REITs routinely operate with loan-to-value ratios between 50% and 65%. Private-equity-backed physician platforms often function at 3.5x to 5.0x EBITDA leverage. None of these entities apologize for leverage. They design it.

Independent physicians, by contrast, are taught to "pay cash when possible" and "stay debt-free." That philosophy guarantees one outcome: you will always be the smallest version of yourself.

I learned that leverage is not theory. It is arithmetic. Let me walk through how I think about it.

When I look at a $10 million ambulatory surgery center real estate project—land, shell, buildout—I do not ask, "Can I afford this?" I ask, "Can this asset afford itself?" A typical bank structure requires 30% equity and 70% debt. That means $3 million of my capital and $7 million of bank capital. At a 6.75% fixed rate amortized over 25 years, annual debt service is approximately $580,000.

If that center stabilizes at $1.5 million in net operating income—and that is not aggressive—the debt service coverage ratio exceeds 2.6x. Most lenders require 1.25x to 1.40x. After paying the bank, the asset throws off roughly $920,000 annually. On a $3 million equity investment, that is over a 30% cash-on-cash return. No appreciation included. No tax strategy included. No refinancing included.

If I paid cash for that same asset, my return drops to 15%. The risk did not go away. The upside did. Leverage did not create danger—it created efficiency.

Then comes appreciation. A conservative 3% annual increase in NOI adds $300,000 in value per year at a 7% cap rate. Over five years, that is $1.5 million in appreciation. On $3 million of equity, that appreciation alone represents a 50% return—before a single dollar of cash flow is counted. This is what leverage does: it compresses time and magnifies equity without requiring additional effort.

I apply the same thinking to equipment. High-cost equipment is where physicians routinely give away ownership out of fear. Take a $3.5 million MRI suite. Financed at 100% over five years at 7%, the monthly payment is roughly $69,000, or $830,000 annually. At 3,000 scans per year—a very achievable number—and a conservative net contribution margin of $325 per scan after staffing, service contracts, and supplies, annual net revenue approaches $975,000. Debt service is covered. Depreciation shelters income. At the end of the note, I own the asset outright.

If I lease that same MRI, I often pay $900,000 to $1 million annually, create zero equity, and hand pricing power to the vendor. Leasing feels safe. Ownership builds empires.

> "The smartest investors are not those who avoid debt, but those who understand exactly how it behaves under stress."
> – Howard Marks

Debt does more than fuel growth—it protects me. Properly structured debt is not exposure; it is insulation. I learned early to separate risk by entity. Real estate lives in one LLC. Operations live in another. Management companies upstream predictable fees. Debt sits at the asset level, often non-recourse. The lender's remedy is the building, not my personal balance sheet.

When reimbursement compresses, labor costs spike, or payer contracts shift, I am not personally destroyed. I renegotiate. I refinance. I reset. Personal guarantees, when unavoidable, are engineered to disappear—burning off after stabilization, capped at fixed amounts, or springing only in cases of fraud. These are not tricks. They are standard structures used by institutional operators every day.

Amortization is the quietest wealth engine I know. On a 25-year amortization schedule, roughly 18% of principal is retired in the first six years and approximately 35% by year ten. On a $7 million loan, that is nearly $2.5 million in equity created without injecting a single additional dollar. The asset pays itself down while I focus on operations and strategy.

Inflation quietly supercharges this process. Fixed-rate debt becomes cheaper every year in real terms. If revenues grow at 4% annually while debt service remains fixed, the real burden of that loan shrinks. A 6.5% fixed-rate loan in a 3–4% inflation environment is not a liability—it is an advantage. I am repaying yesterday's dollars with tomorrow's revenue.

Debt also gives me optionality. Once an asset stabilizes, I can refinance. A project initially capitalized at a 7.75% cap rate can refinance at 6.25% after optimization and market normalization. On a $10 million asset, that cap-rate compression alone can unlock $2–3 million in additional value. Refinancing often allows me to extract 60–80% of my original equity tax-free while retaining ownership and cash flow. That is how portfolios scale without constant capital calls.

Most importantly, debt gives me control over timing. I do not have to sell when markets are weak. I refinance. I extend maturities. I adjust amortization. Equity-only operators are forced sellers. Debt-structured operators choose liquidity events.

I also design debt for failure—not because I expect it, but because I respect reality. Healthcare is cyclical. Payor mixes shift. Labor markets tighten. Regulations change. When a center underperforms, equity-only investors panic. Debt-structured entities renegotiate terms or walk away from a single asset without detonating the entire platform. That is not failure. That is controlled retreat.

Physicians are trained to eliminate risk, not to price it. But risk does not disappear when I avoid leverage—it transforms into opportunity cost. Avoiding debt feels safe. Safety does not compound.

The final lesson I learned is simple: equity without leverage is labor-dependent wealth. It requires my constant presence and constant output. Equity paired with disciplined, asset-level debt becomes architecture. It allows time, amortization, inflation, and refinancing to do the heavy lifting. It allows mistakes without ruin and success without exhaustion.

I did not build scale by writing checks. I built it by designing debt—carefully, deliberately, and without apology. As Warren Buffett said, " The use of debt is like a razor: in the right hands it is a useful tool; in the wrong hands it can be fatal."

CHAPTER 13

WHEN THE MATH BREAKS: USING CHAPTER 11 AS A STRATEGIC RESET

"When the facts change, I change my mind.
What do you do, sir?"
– John Maynard Keynes

Not every plan works. Not every market behaves. Not every partnership survives contact with reality. One of the most dangerous myths in business—especially in healthcare—is the belief that success is measured only by growth. Durability matters just as much. Knowing how to unwind a business intelligently is as important as knowing how to build one.

That is why this book ends with a topic most people avoid until they are forced into it: controlled failure.

"In the middle of difficulty lies opportunity."
– Albert Einstein

Several years ago, a hospital owner reached out to me with a proposal that illustrates this concept perfectly. His hospital was not collapsing. It was operating. Revenues existed. Patients were coming through the doors. But creditors were tightening, flexibility was disappearing, and the capital structure no longer made sense. The margins for error had vanished. His response was not panic. It was Chapter 11.

That conversation is worth unpacking, because it demonstrates how restructuring—and Chapter 11 in particular—can be used as a strategic exit vehicle when the math no longer works.

What he was describing was not a "we're broke" bankruptcy. It was a deliberate bankruptcy paired with a conversion strategy. A reset, not a surrender.

The sequence was straightforward. First, the hospital would file for Chapter 11. That filing immediately triggers an automatic stay, freezing creditor actions such as lawsuits, collections, and foreclosures. It forces every counterparty to stop and come to the table. Inside Chapter 11, management typically remains in control as the debtor in possession, allowing operations to continue while leverage shifts. Debt can be rejected, renegotiated, or crammed down. Contracts that once felt immovable suddenly become negotiable.

Second, the balance sheet gets cleaned up inside the bankruptcy process. Unsecured debt can be reduced or discharged. Secured debt can be restructured. Long-term vendor contracts, legacy obligations, litigation exposure, and even pension-related liabilities can be addressed in an orderly way. The goal is not destruction. It is simplification.

Third—and this was the real endgame—the hospital would be converted from a for-profit entity into a not-for-profit institution. This conversion often occurs during or immediately after bankruptcy, when assets can be transferred at a distressed valuation. In practical terms, the hospital is sold or donated to a newly formed nonprofit entity, emerging with a dramatically different posture.

In short, Chapter 11 becomes a reset button. It neutralizes creditor pressure and allows the business to re-emerge in a structure that is harder to attack and easier to support going forward.

The question, of course, is why convert from for-profit to not-for-profit at all?

A not-for-profit hospital carries structural advantages that for-profit hospitals simply do not. From a legal standpoint, nonprofits have no owners or shareholders—only a governing board. Once assets are properly transferred, they are generally insulated from private creditors. Historical claims become far harder to pursue, particularly when the conversion is executed through bankruptcy court oversight.

The tax advantages are significant. Not-for-profit hospitals pay no federal income tax, usually no state income tax, and often no property tax. Sales and use tax exemptions frequently apply as well. These are not minor details; they change the entire economics of survival.

Revenue dynamics shift too. Nonprofits have better access to government grants, philanthropy, and donations. They can tap municipal bond markets through tax-exempt financing. They are often better positioned to receive Medicaid supplemental payments, Disproportionate Share Hospital funds, and state or local subsidies. The same hospital, with the same walls and the same patients, suddenly operates under a very different financial gravity.

There is also political and regulatory cover. The "community benefit" framing changes the conversation. Regulators, legislators, and municipalities tend to treat nonprofit hospitals as essential public assets rather than businesses that simply miscalculated leverage.

At this point, the obvious question arose for me, and you: how does the original owner still benefit if the hospital is "not for profit"?

This is the part that is rarely discussed openly. While nonprofits have no owners, control and economics do not disappear. They relocate.

Control often begins with governance. Founders typically appoint the initial board. They may remain CEO, president, medical director, or all three. Board seats are not ceremonial; they are power.

Management is another lever. A separate for-profit management company—often owned by the former owner or affiliates—can provide administration, billing, IT, and facilities management. The nonprofit pays ongoing management fees. Profit does not vanish; it changes form.

Real estate is frequently separated as well. The hospital building is owned by a for-profit real estate entity, while the nonprofit signs a long-term lease. Rent payments continue regardless of nonprofit status. This structure alone can represent the majority of economic upside.

Compensation is another mechanism. Nonprofit executives can be paid very well as long as compensation is deemed reasonable. This is how seven-figure nonprofit hospital CEOs legally exist.

Finally, influence remains over future transactions—mergers, affiliations, asset sales, and joint ventures. Equity disappears. Control does not.

That said, caution is essential. Investors cannot invest in a nonprofit hospital in the traditional sense. There is no stock. No ownership. No dividends. No exit. When someone says they want to "bring investors into a nonprofit hospital," what they usually mean is something else.

In reality, capital comes in around the nonprofit, not into it.

The cleanest structure is real estate investment. Investors fund or acquire the hospital property and lease it to the nonprofit, receiving predictable rental income.

Another common approach is investing in the for-profit management company that holds a long-term contract with the nonprofit. Cash flow comes from management fees, not hospital ownership.

Joint ventures outside the hospital are also common—surgery centers, imaging centers, labs, and specialty service lines. These remain for-profit and feed volume into the nonprofit hospital.

Some arrangements take the form of debt marketed as "impact investing"—loans, notes, bonds, or program-related investments. Returns are capped but steady.

Others are philanthropic plays. Large donors receive board seats, naming rights, and strategic influence. The return is not financial; it is power, prestige, and access.

There are clear red flags in all of this. Anyone pitching "ownership" in a nonprofit hospital. Promises of equity-like returns. Vague explanations about structures that will be figured out later. Blurred lines between nonprofit entities, for-profit affiliates, and personal compensation. These are classic setups for IRS scrutiny, state attorney general intervention, governance disasters, and investor lawsuits.

The bottom line is this: the hospital owner was not trying to disappear. He was trying to reposition. Bankruptcy was the tool, not the destination. The nonprofit structure was the shield, not the sacrifice. Capital would be raised around the institution, not inside it.

Chapter 11 is often misunderstood as defeat. In reality, it is a legal pause button. It freezes creditor action, forces renegotiation, and preserves value when used correctly. More importantly, it creates time to redesign the business.

In healthcare, this strategy is particularly powerful because assets do not vanish when margins compress. Patients still come. Payors still pay. Facilities still matter. Chapter 11 simply realigns who gets paid, when, and under what rules.

The lesson is uncomfortable but essential. Smart operators do not just plan for upside. They plan for exits that preserve dignity, control, and optionality. If growth stalls, leverage tightens, or partners misalign, knowing how to unwind cleanly is a form of power.

Wealth is not built solely by knowing how to win.

It is built by knowing how not to lose. As Sun Tzu once said, " He who knows when he can fight and when he cannot will be victorious."

EPILOGUE

"The man who works for wages works only for a part of the day; the rest of the day he works for another man."
– Abraham Lincoln

I used to believe the path to wealth was paved with hard work and high-level clinical precision. For years, I operated under the assumption that if I just did more, billed more, and stayed focused on the technical aspects of my practice, the financial result would naturally take care of itself. I sat in the physician's chair, content in my role, viewing my high income as the ultimate scoreboard. I thought I was winning the game because my bank account was growing, but I was fundamentally blind to the fact that I wasn't actually playing the game—I was the equipment being used by the people who truly owned it.

This realization didn't hit me in a boardroom; it hit me during a quiet moment of exhaustion when I looked at the system and finally saw the "value stack" for what it really was. I saw that wealth isn't about how much you earn; it's about how much you own and how much leverage you control. In healthcare, we are meticulously trained to be elite laborers, but we are never taught how to be architects of our own equity. We are taught to be the product, and products, by definition, are depreciating assets that can eventually be replaced or phased out by the next model.

This book is the culmination of my personal shift from a clinical mindset to an ownership mindset. It is not a collection of vague theories or a list of stocks to buy. Instead, it is a map of the hidden terrain where real capital moves. I want to show you how to stop looking at your career through the narrow lens of a salary and start seeing it as a platform for building durable, systemic wealth. We are going to dismantle the "labor stack" that keeps you on the treadmill and replace it with a strategic framework that puts you in the owner's suite.

It's time to stop being the revenue and start being the person who controls the flow. It's time to stop running and start building.

Qui tenet clavem, tenet regnum.
He who holds the key, holds the kingdom.
